TEEN RIGHTS AND FREEDOMS

| Free
Press

TEEN RIGHTS AND FREEDOMS

Free Press

Sylvia Engdahl
Book Editor

GREENHAVEN PRESS
A part of Gale, Cengage Learning

GALE
CENGAGE Learning·

Detroit • New York • San Francisco • New Haven, Conn • Waterville, Maine • London

Elizabeth Des Chenes, *Managing Editor*

© 2012 Greenhaven Press, a part of Gale, Cengage Learning

For more information, contact:
Greenhaven Press
27500 Drake Rd.
Farmington Hills, MI 48331-3535
Or you can visit our Internet site at gale.cengage.com.

For product information and technology assistance, contact us at:

Gale Customer Support, 1-800-877-4253.
For permission to use material from this text or product, submit all requests online at www.cengage.com/permissions.

Further permissions questions can be emailed to permissionrequest@cengage.com.

Articles in Greenhaven Press anthologies are often edited for length to meet page requirements. In addition, original titles of these works are changed to clearly present the main thesis and to explicitly indicate the author's opinion. Every effort is made to ensure the Greenhaven Press accurately reflects the original intent of the authors. Every effort has been made to trace the owners of copyrighted material.

Cover Image © Hill Street Studios/Blend Images/Getty Images

LIBRARY OF CONGRESS CATALOGING-IN-PUBLICATION DATA

Free press / Sylvia Engdahl, book editor.
 p. cm. -- (Teen rights and freedoms)
 Includes bibliographical references and index.
 ISBN 978-0-7377-5827-6 (hardcover)
1. Student newspapers and periodicals--Law and legislation--United States.
2. Student newspapers and periodicals--Censorship--United States. 3. Freedom of the press--United States. I. Engdahl, Sylvia.
 KF4165.F74 2011
 342.7308'53--dc23

                                                                    2011020812

Printed in the United States of America
1 2 3 4 5 6 7 15 14 13 12 11

Contents

   The Supreme Court has decided only three cases relevant to freedom of the press for high school students: *Tinker v. Des Moines* (1969), *Bethel School District v. Fraser* (1986), and *Hazelwood v. Kuhlmeier* (1988). These rulings still determine how much censorship is allowed.

   The US District Court's Decision

   Charles Metzner

   In the first court case involving a high school newspaper, the judge rules that the principal of a high school in New York state violated the First Amendment by prohibiting students from accepting a paid advertisement opposing the Vietnam War.

   The Supreme Court's Decision

   Byron White

   In *Hazelwood v. Kuhlmeier* the Supreme Court rules that schools have a right to control student publications that are associated with an activity that is part of the school curriculum.

A journalism professor points out that it is not enough to educate high school students and advisers about freedom of the press for high schools when it is the administrators who are behind the censorship.

he does not have, as what he writes is printed only at the discretion of the owner of the newspaper he works for.

Kenneth Dautrich, David A. Yalof, and Mark Jose López

Professors of political science report results of a study of high school students' attitudes toward First Amendment rights. They found that many students think there is too much freedom of expression, but that those who use digital media such as blogs are less likely to think so than other students.

Foreword

*"In the truest sense freedom cannot be
bestowed, it must be achieved."*
Franklin D. Roosevelt,
September 16, 1936

The notion of children and teens having rights is a relatively recent development. Early in American history, the head of the household—nearly always the father—exercised complete control over the children in the family. Children were legally considered to be the property of their parents. Over time, this view changed, as society began to acknowledge that children have rights independent of their parents, and that the law should protect young people from exploitation. By the early twentieth century, more and more social reformers focused on the welfare of children, and over the ensuing decades advocates worked to protect them from harm in the workplace, to secure public education for all, and to guarantee fair treatment for youths in the criminal justice system. Throughout the twentieth century, rights for children and teens—and restrictions on those rights—were established by Congress and reinforced by the courts. Today's courts are still defining and clarifying the rights and freedoms of young people, sometimes expanding those rights and sometimes limiting them. Some teen rights are outside the scope of public law and remain in the realm of the family, while still others are determined by school policies.

Each volume in the Teen Rights and Freedoms series focuses on a different right or freedom and offers an anthology of key essays and articles on that right or freedom and the responsibilities that come with it. Material within each volume is drawn from a diverse selection of primary and secondary sources— journals, magazines, newspapers, nonfiction books, organization newsletters, position papers, speeches, and government documents, with a particular emphasis on Supreme Court and lower court decisions. Volumes also include first-person narratives from young people and others involved in teen rights issues, such as parents and educators. The material is selected and arranged to highlight all the major social and legal controversies relating to the right or freedom under discussion. Each selection is preceded by an introduction that provides context and background. In many cases, the essays point to the difference between adult and teen rights, and why this difference exists.

Many of the volumes cover rights guaranteed under the Bill of Rights and how these rights are interpreted and protected in regard to children and teens, including freedom of speech, freedom of the press, due process, and religious rights. The scope of the series also encompasses rights or freedoms, whether real or perceived, relating to the school environment, such as electronic devices, dress, Internet policies, and privacy. Some volumes focus on the home environment, including topics such as parental control and sexuality.

Numerous features are included in each volume of Teen Rights and Freedoms:

- An annotated **table of contents** provides a brief summary of each essay in the volume and highlights court decisions and personal narratives.

- An **introduction** specific to the volume topic gives context for the right or freedom and its impact on daily life.

- A brief **chronology** offers important dates associated with the right or freedom, including landmark court cases.

- **Primary sources**—including personal narratives and court decisions—are among the varied selections in the anthology.

- **Illustrations**—including photographs, charts, graphs, tables, statistics, and maps—are closely tied to the text and chosen to help readers understand key points or concepts.

- An annotated list of **organizations to contact** presents sources of additional information on the topic.
- A **for further reading** section offers a bibliography of books, periodical articles, and Internet sources for further research.
- A comprehensive subject **index** provides access to key people, places, events, and subjects cited in the text.

Each volume of Teen Rights and Freedoms delves deeply into the issues most relevant to the lives of teens: their own rights, freedoms, and responsibilities. With the help of this series, students and other readers can explore from many angles the evolution and current expression of rights both historic and contemporary.

Introduction

Of the constitutional rights possessed by Americans, freedom of the press is among the least often mentioned by people asked to name them. In a 2010 survey, only 18 percent thought of it, as opposed to 61 percent who knew that the First Amendment guarantees freedom of speech. The fact that in the United States anyone with the money to publish or otherwise disseminate ideas can do so without being stopped by the government is simply taken for granted by many. Yet at the time the Constitution was written, allowing a free press was an exception to the situation elsewhere in the world, and there are still countries where no such right exists. A free press is vital to the preservation of democracy. Without it—without an inviolable right to spread news and opinion more widely than among an individual's personal contacts—effective criticism of government policies would not be possible.

Legally, there is little difference between freedom of speech and freedom of the press; both are covered by the Constitution's First Amendment, and most Supreme Court justices have believed that there is no need to distinguish between them. In *First National Bank of Boston v. Bellotti* (1978) Chief Justice Warren E. Burger wrote, "Because the First Amendment was meant to guarantee freedom to express and communicate ideas, I can see no difference between the right of those who seek to disseminate ideas by way of a newspaper and those who give lectures or speeches and seek to enlarge the audience by publication and wide dissemination." In practice, however, there can be a difference between use of communications media and in-person communication; for example, a government could allow citizens to speak freely yet shut down unauthorized printing presses, and a school may allow students to speak their opinions but not allow them to print unapproved articles in the school newspaper. So the fact that the press is specifically mentioned in the Amendment does matter.

People often misunderstand the First Amendment. Freedom of speech does not mean that anyone can say whatever he or she wants anywhere, under any circumstances; and freedom of the press does not mean that reporters and editors can publish whatever they wish in newspapers or through other media. Rather, it means that the *government* cannot prevent them from doing so (except in a few special situations mentioned below). The Constitution is about what the government can, and cannot, do. It does not control the actions of private organizations or individuals.

In the world of professional journalism—and of all mass media—authors, unless they self-publish at their own expense, cannot present their work to the public unless it is accepted by an editor. Editors, for their part, cannot accept anything objectionable to the owner of the publication they work for; they can be fired if they do so, and that sometimes happens. Such an outcome is not a violation of their First Amendment rights. Why, then, do students have a First Amendment right to express their views in public school newspapers without censorship by the administration? It is because public schools are government organizations, and school administrators and teachers are therefore considered government officials. They cannot legally impose as many rules as the administrators of private schools can; they are bound by the Constitution's restrictions on government power.

Not everyone believes that schools should be considered "government" in that sense—their administrators function not as officials but as educators, and some people feel that it is their job to see that students act in ways acceptable to the community, as well as to protect younger children from material they are not mature enough to understand. After all, laws often recognize a distinction between minors and adults. The Supreme Court ruled, in the 1969 landmark case *Tinker v. Des Moines Independent Community School District*, that with very few exceptions minor students have the same First Amendment rights as adults, but there has always been some disagreement with that decision, which was not unanimous; and in a later case, *Hazelwood School District v. Kuhlmeier,* the number of exceptions was increased. *Hazelwood,* though controversial, was met with approval by many. The *Chicago Tribune* wrote on January 15, 1988:

> We now have a decision that says 1st Amendment rights are suspended and censorship allowed when school newspapers are part of the curriculum. . . . What the court should have said is that 1st Amendment rights to expression without censorship do not extend to editor-publisher relationships. No editors in our history have had a constitutionally guaranteed right to publish something in a newspaper that the publishers did not want in there. Editors who can't agree with publishers have to find a new job or become publishers themselves.
>
> In this case the students and their journalism teacher are, in practice, the editors; the public, through the school board and its agent, the principal, is the publisher. If the editors don't put out a newspaper with which the publisher agrees, they can express their First Amendment rights by producing some newspaper off the publicly owned premises, one for which the school board does not have the ultimate liability.

Defenders of freedom of the press for students, however, believe that there is good reason for public schools to be viewed as the government rather than as publishers. They hold that it is important to bar *any* form of government from placing limits on what people can write or read—and that this is as true in the case of young people as of adults, if not more so. In totalitarian countries, the government usually enforces such limits, and historically, totalitarian rulers have often established and maintained their power by controlling what was taught in the schools. They have dictated not only what students could write, but what books they could read, and rebels have been punished not by suspension from school but by imprisonment or even death. This may seem irrelevant because the United States does not have a totalitarian government, but the authors of the Constitution and its amendments wrote them in order to guarantee that it would never have one. All provisions of the amendments known as the Bill of Rights were considered necessary to ensure the long-term freedom of US citizens.

To be sure, some governmental restrictions on freedom of the press and other media do exist and have been found constitutional—laws prohibiting obscenity, child pornography, incitement to illegal acts, disclosure of information affecting national security, or libel, for instance. Most people agree that these are essential to the functioning of society. It is also against the law to reproduce copyrighted material without permission; the government regulates the use of radio and TV broadcast frequencies; and in some cases there are conditions attached to the use of public funds. None of these special situations involve the suppression of ideas or personal opinions.

Sometimes, however, people feel that their opinions have been censored when that is not the case. Censorship is another concept that is frequently misunderstood. The mere selection of material to be made available is not censorship. Most obviously, it is not censorship when a piece of writing is rejected for publication because of poor grammar and spelling. Beyond that, editors must select the best work to publish when there is not room for all submissions—just as librarians must select the best books for the library when they cannot buy all that exist. It is their legitimate responsibility to decide what is best. Censorship exists only when something of acceptable quality is banned from publication or display, or removed from the library, *because of* content considered objectionable. Americans have a constitutional right to be free of censorship, but they have no right to force others to disseminate their work.

The censorship of the work of student journalists is a highly controversial issue at present. Many public school administrators believe it is necessary and proper to censor what is distributed on campus, and they do not see this activity as a violation of students' rights. Some states have laws declaring that it is, but most do not. Furthermore, federal courts do not agree about the extent of those rights in the case of students. There have been many lawsuits dealing with student publications, and not all have been decided in the students' favor. One case, *R.O. v. Ithaca City School District* (dealt with in the last two viewpoints in this book), has not yet been settled as this book goes to press; however it turns out, its outcome is likely to influence schools across the United States.

Chronology

1943
In *West Virginia State Board of Education v. Barnette* the Supreme Court for the first time clearly recognizes that the First Amendment protects public school students by ruling that they have the right to refuse to say the Pledge of Allegiance.

1969
In *Tinker v. Des Moines* the Supreme Court rules that students have a constitutional right to free speech in public schools as long as it does not disrupt classwork or create substantial disorder. This principle becomes known as the Tinker standard.

1969
Zucker v. Panitz, the first case to apply the Tinker standard to student media, is decided by a federal district court, which rules that a school newspaper must be allowed to publish an ad protesting the war in Vietnam.

1974
The Student Press Law Center, a nonprofit agency, is established to educate journalism students and teachers about their right to freedom of the press and provide free legal advice when that right is violated.

1977
California becomes the first state in the nation to pass a law specifically grant-

ing freedom of the press to public high school students.

1988   In *Hazelwood v. Kuhlmeier* the Supreme Court rules that schools may censor school-sponsored student publications as long as the censorship is reasonably related to legitimate educational concerns, except when the publication is a public forum.

1988   Massachusetts becomes the first state to enact a student free expression law guaranteeing more freedom than federal law in response to the *Hazelwood v. Kuhlmeier* ruling. Since then, six other states have done so.

2002   The American Society of Newspaper Editors launches My High School Journalism, a hosting service for high school newspapers, to encourage the growing trend of putting them online.

2005   In *Hosty v. Carter*, the Seventh US Circuit Court of Appeals extends *Hazelwood v. Kuhlmeier* to college newspapers by ruling that they can be censored unless determined to be public forums. This may affect high school newspapers by reinforcing the requirement that a court must go through careful public forum analysis whenever a school claims that *Hazelwood* justifies censorship.

2008   California amends its student free expression law to protect journalism teachers from being fired or reassigned for allowing students to publish controversial stories.

"The Hazelwood decision was clearly a defeat for student free speech rights. School officials were now allowed to censor school newspapers."

Supreme Court Rulings Have Shaped Freedom of the Press for Student Journalists

The following anonymously authored article from an encyclopedia of law explains the Supreme Court decisions that determine how much freedom of the press students are allowed. Although two of the cases, Tinker v. Des Moines *and* Bethel v. Fraser, *dealt with free speech issues rather than with the press, they are nevertheless used by courts as precedents that apply to student publications. It is important to be aware that these Supreme Court rulings apply only to public school students, as the First Amendment affects only what the government can and cannot do—private schools administrators can censor anything they wish unless restricted by a state law.*

Sixty years ago, when the U.S. Supreme Court decided its first free speech case involving students and the public schools, the idea that students had any right to free speech would have been considered laughable at best, dangerous at worst. At that time, school was considered a privilege to attend, and rules or

"Education: Student Rights/Free Speech," *Gale Encyclopedia of Everyday Law*, 2nd. Ed., Detroit, MI: Gale, 2006, 501–503. Copyright © 2006 by Gale, a part of Cengage Learning, Inc. Adapted from the original and reproduced by permission. www.cengage.com/permissions.

regulations the school sought to enforce were untouchable. This generalization was collectively true at the elementary, secondary and college levels of education.

Student rights to free speech did not really become an issue until the Vietnam War, when more and more students found themselves at opposite ends of the political spectrum from their teachers and school administrators. The Supreme Court's 1969 decision in *Tinker v. Des Moines Independent School District* opened the floodgates to school free speech litigation, and while court decisions have certainly gone back and forth between the right to free speech and the need to impose discipline and respect the feelings of all students, there has never been any attempt to go back to the strict free speech restrictions of the pre-Vietnam War era.

Public school free speech rights for students can be divided into those applying to elementary and secondary students and those dealing with college issues. Since college students are adults, the First Amendment situations dealt with are substantially different. Analyzing student free speech rights in this way can give a cohesive picture of those rights for students today.

Free Speech Rights in Public Schools

Free speech rights in public elementary and secondary schools have undergone a remarkable transformation in the past 30 years, from nonexistence to a perpetual tension between those rights and the need for schools to control student behavior in order to preserve the sanctity of the learning environment. Today, it would be most accurate to say that public schools students have some First Amendment rights in schools, but certainly not as many as adults do in the real world. Although *Tinker v. Des Moines Independent School District* was the landmark case that set forth the standards [by] which current student free speech cases are judged, the first case that suggested students had some First Amendment rights was decided much earlier [in the 1943 case *West Virginia State Board of Education v. Barnette*, where

What Is Meant by the Term "Free Press"?

The First Amendment says "Congress shall make no law . . . abridging the freedom . . . of the press." Under the Due Process Clause of the Fourteenth Amendment, states also must recognize freedom of the press.

When the United States adopted the First Amendment in 1791, the press meant printed books, newspapers, and pamphlets, also called handbills. With advances in technology, the press came to include the broadcast media of radio and television. In the 1990s the Internet expanded the press to include computer-based publications.

The freedom of the press protects the right to publish information and to express ideas in these various media. It is an important right in a free society. To make sure government is running properly, citizens need to be informed. People do not have the time or ability to watch everything the government does. The press serves this function by investigating and reporting on the government's activity. . . .

Censorship is sometimes called "prior restraint" because it keeps a publication from being printed. In the case of *Near v. Minnesota* (1931), the U.S. Supreme Court officially ruled that the First Amendment prohibits the government from using prior restraint. . . .

The Supreme Court, however, has recognized a number of exceptions to the rule against prior restraints. The government may ban the printing of obscene material, which is sexual material that is offensive. The Supreme Court says obscenity is not protected by the First Amendment because it has no value in the flow of information in society.

"Freedom of the Press," Supreme Court
Drama: Cases That Changed America, *Ed.
Daniel Brannen, Richard Hanes, and Elizabeth
Shaw, vol. 1, Detroit: U*X*L, 2001. 29–34. Gale
Virtual Reference Library.*

several students and their parents challenged the West Virginia State Board of Education's mandate that they salute the flag and recite the Pledge of Allegiance. The students and parents ultimately won the case.] . . .

Tinker v. Des Moines Independent Community School District The case of *Tinker v. Des Moines Independent Community School District* in 1969 shattered the peace and made sure there would be controversy for a long time to come. The Vietnam War was raging full force when the students at a Des Moines, Iowa, high school decided to wear black armbands to school one day to protest what they saw as an unjust struggle. The school administrators learned of their plan and passed a rule banning black armbands from the school and suspending any student caught wearing one. The students wore the armbands anyway, and as a result were suspended. They sued the school district.

In writing in favor of the students for the majority, Justice Abe Fortas wrote these iconic words:

> It can hardly be argued that either students or teachers shed their constitutional rights to freedom of speech or expression at the schoolhouse gate . . . School officials do not possess absolute authority over their students. Students in school as well as out of school are 'persons' under our Constitution. They are possessed of fundamental rights which the State must respect. . . . In the absence of specific showing of constitutionally valid reasons to regulate their speech, students are entitled to freedom of expression of their views.

But Fortas added an important caveat: conduct that "materially disrupts classwork or involves substantial disorder or invasion of the rights of others is, of course, not immunized by the constitutional guarantee of freedom of speech." In other words, not all student conduct is First Amendment protected, only that which does not disturb the classroom environment or invade the rights of others. This standard, also known as the "material and substantial disruption test," has basically remained the standard

A student at Antioch High School in Antioch, Illinois, stands before her journalism class. Student behavior has been molded by several court rulings spanning over thirty years. © Stacey Wescott/Chicago Tibune/MCT/MCT via Getty Images.

in which the school's right to proscribe free speech is examined at the secondary rank as well as at public colleges and universities.

After Tinker, a host of cases were brought at the lower court level litigating public school free speech issues. Many of these came down on the side of freedom of expression for students. Many lower courts found themselves asking, after *Tinker*, what student speech can in fact be regulated.

Bethel School District No. 403 v. Fraser The Supreme Court finally attempted to set some limits on student First Amendment rights in the 1986 case of *Bethel School District No. 403 v. Fraser*. Matthew Fraser made a speech . . . full of obscenities and innuendoes [at a school assembly]. When school officials attempted to discipline him for his speech, he sued. The Supreme Court sided with the school.

The Court found that Fraser had failed the "substantial disorder" part of the *Tinker* test. Chief Justice Warren Burger, writing for the majority, said that schools have a responsibility to instill students with "habits and manners of civility as values." The effect of Fraser's speech, suggested Burger, was to undermine this responsibility; therefore, he did not receive First Amendment protection for it. Not only can schools take into account whether speech is offensive to other students, said Burger, "the undoubted freedom to advocate unpopular and controversial views in schools and classrooms must be balanced against the society's countervailing interest in teaching students the boundaries of socially appropriate behavior." *Bethel* served notice that the Supreme Court saw limitations on student free speech rights. The next big school First Amendment case decided by the court served to emphasize that point.

Hazelwood School District v. Kuhlmeier The school newspaper at Hazelwood East High School in Missouri was courting controversy when it decided to publish an article on pregnancy among students naming names, as well as an article on students of divorced parents. The principal of the school censored both articles from the school paper. The student editors of the newspaper sued.

In 1988, the Supreme Court handed down its decision: a complete defeat for the students. The majority of the court claimed *Tinker* did not apply to this case, since the school newspaper was a school-sponsored activity. According to the Court, when an activity is school sponsored, school officials may censor speech as long as such censorship is reasonably related to legitimate educational concerns. The Court went on to define these concerns broadly, stating that school officials would have the right to censor material that is "ungrammatical, poorly written, inadequately researched, biased or prejudiced, vulgar or profane, or unsuitable for immature audiences, or inconsistent with shared values of a civilized social order."

Hazelwood did distinguish between school-sponsored publications and other activities, and publications and activities that were not school sponsored, which the Court suggested would be given greater free-speech leeway. Nevertheless, the *Hazelwood* decision was clearly a defeat for student free speech rights. School officials were now allowed to censor school newspapers, as well as other school-sponsored activities such as theatrical productions, in "any reasonable manner."

Elementary and Secondary Student Rights Since Hazelwood

[As of 2003] since *Hazelwood*, the Supreme Court has not tackled a non-religious free speech issue involving a public elementary or high school. Lower courts that have dealt with these issues have tended to follow *Hazelwood*'s ruling pretty closely: if a free speech case involves a school-sponsored activity, school officials are given wide latitude. Since all but a few student free speech cases involve a school-sponsored activity, the effect has been that most free speech cases have gone against students, with some minor exceptions.

Lower courts have also determined that school officials have broad discretion at the elementary school level in controlling student speech, ruling in several cases that *Tinker* does not apply. However, most legal commentators believe that despite these developments, *Tinker* still remains in force, at least for high school students. School administrators are still required to show "material and substantial disruption" before limiting student speech in non–school-sponsored activities.

Higher Education Free Speech Issues

Institutions of higher education have generally been held to have less control over student free speech rights than elementary and high school teachers and administrators. In part, this position reflects the fact that college students are adults. However, there have still been areas of controversy in post-secondary student free speech rights, generally having to do with funding issues. The latest area of controversy has been with so-called "hate codes," which ban . . . [from college campuses] certain types of speech considered offensive.

> "It is patently unfair in light of the free
> speech doctrine to close to the students
> the forum which they deem effective to
> present their ideas."

Student Newspapers Must Be Allowed to Publish Controversial Paid Ads

The US District Court's Decision

Charles Metzner

In the following opinion Charles Metzner, a judge of the US District Court for the Southern District of New York, rules that the principal of New Rochelle High School was wrong in not allowing the editors of the school paper to publish an ad protesting the Vietnam War. He points out that although the school argued that the paper was supposed to cover only school activities, it had often published articles about the war, the draft, and other controversial issues, and there was no logical reason to prohibit ads on subjects dealt with by news stories. This was the first case involving the student press ever taken to court.

Charles Metzner, Court's opinion, *Zucker v. Panitz*, US District Court for the Southern District of New York, May 15, 1969.

This action concerns the right of high school students to publish a paid advertisement opposing the war in Vietnam in their school newspaper. The action is brought . . . by the principal of New Rochelle High School, the president of the New Rochelle Board of Education, and the New Rochelle Superintendent of Schools. . . .

A group of New Rochelle High School students, led by plaintiff Richard Orentzel, formed an Ad Hoc Student Committee Against the War in Vietnam. The group sought to publish an advertisement in opposition to the war in the student newspaper, the *Huguenot Herald*, in November 1967, offering to pay the standard student rate. The text of the proposed advertisement is as follows: "The United States government is pursuing a policy in Viet Nam which is both repugnant to moral and international law and dangerous to the future of humanity. We can stop it. We must stop it." The editorial board of the newspaper, which was then headed by plaintiff Laura Zucker, approved publication of the advertisement, but the principal of the school, Dr. Adolph Panitz, directed that the advertisement not be published. The affidavit of plaintiff Orentzel alleges that the committee still desires to publish the advertisement and has been informed that the newspaper would accept it but for the directive of the principal.

The gravamen [significant part] of the dispute concerns the function and content of the school newspaper. Plaintiffs allege that the purpose of the *Huguenot Herald* is inter alia [among other things] "to provide a forum for the dissemination of ideas and information by and to the students of New Rochelle High School." Therefore, prohibition of the advertisement constitutes a constitutionally proscribed abridgement of their freedom of speech.

The defendants take issue with this characterization of the newspaper. They advance the theory that the publication "is not a newspaper in the usual sense" but is a "beneficial educational device" developed as part of the curriculum and intended to inure primarily to the benefit of those who compile, edit and publish it." They assert a longstanding policy of the school administration which limits news items and editorials to matters pertaining to the high school and its activities. Similarly, "no advertising will be permitted which expresses a point of view on any subject not related to New Rochelle High School." Even paid advertising in support of student government nominees is prohibited and only purely commercial advertising is accepted. This policy is alleged to be reasonable and necessary to preserve the journal as an educational device and prevent it from becoming mainly an organ for the dissemination of news and views unrelated to the high school.

In sum, defendants' main factual argument is that the war is not a school-related activity, and therefore not qualified for news, editorial and advertising treatment. They have submitted issues of the newspaper from September 1968 to April 1969 to illustrate school-related subjects and the absence of other than purely commercial advertising.

The School Newspaper Covered Controversial Topics

If the *Huguenot Herald*'s contents were truly as flaccid as the defendants' argument implies, it would indeed be a sterile publication. Furthermore, its function as an educational device surely could not be served if such were the content of the paper. However, it is clear that the newspaper is more than a mere activity time and place sheet. The factual core of defendants' argument falls with a perusal of the newspapers submitted to the court. They illustrate that the newspaper is being used as a communications [medium] regarding controversial topics and that the teaching of journalism includes dissemination of such ideas. Such a school paper is truly an educational device.

For instance, on October 18, 1968, an article on draft board procedures, including discussion of the basis for graduate deferments as well as problems of initial registration appeared, as well as an article concerning a poll of high school students on national political candidates and the war. On January 31, 1969, the paper

Some Controversial Ads Can Be Banned from Student Publications

In 1978 the principal of Springbrook High School in Montgomery County, Maryland, prohibited distribution of an issue of the student underground newspaper Joint Effort *because it contained a paid advertisement for drug paraphernalia. The students filed a lawsuit alleging that this act interfered with their First Amendment rights. The lower court ruled for the school, so the students appealed; but the US Court of Appeals upheld the ruling. The following passage is a portion of its opinion.*

We find no merit to the argument that a reasonably intelligent high school student would not know that an advertisement promoting the sale of drug paraphernalia encourages actions that endanger the health or safety of students. . . . The First Amendment rights of the students must yield to the superior interest of the school in seeing that materials that encourage actions which endanger the health or safety of students are not distributed on school property. . . .

We also find no merit to the argument of plaintiffs that the school officials had to demonstrate that the material would substantially disrupt school activities. . . . Such disruption . . . is merely one justification for school authorities to restrain the distribution of a publication; nowhere has it been held to be the sole justification. . . .

Finally, we think the fact that the advertisement was purely commercial is an additional reason for upholding the prohibition against distributing the *Joint Effort* on school property. Commercial speech, although protected by the First Amendment, is not entitled to the same degree of protection as other types of speech. This case is quite different from one, for example, in which a school prohibits the distribution of a publication containing an article of some literary value that may examine drugs and drug use. The printed material in issue here was paid for by a store seeking to profit from its encouragement of the use of drugs.

included an item that the principal had placed literature on the draft in the school library. On April 25, 1969, the paper reported on a draft information assembly and informed its readers of the availability of draft counseling outside the school. Moreover, items have appeared on the following: the grant of money by the students' General Organization to Eldridge Cleaver to speak at Iona College (vetoed by the principal); school fundraising activities for Biafra; federal aid for preschool through high school education; meeting of a YMCA-sponsored group whose purpose is discussion of such issues as racial change, violence and political action possibilities; a state assemblyman's proposal for an elected Board of Education; the proposal of several educators for community involvement as part of the educational process; types of narcotics and their effects; high school drug use; community treatment facilities; establishment of a new anti-Establishment high school newspaper; and a letter to the editor that a poll should be held to determine whether the newspaper should serve more than its present function and become an instrument and advocate of student power.

The presence of articles concerning the draft and student opinion of United States participation in the war shows that the war is considered to be a school-related subject. This being the case, there is no logical reason to permit news stories on the subject and preclude student advertising.

Defendants further argue that since no advertising on political matters in permitted, the plaintiffs have no cause for discontent. It is undisputed that no such advertising has been permitted, but this is not dispositive [related to the case]. In *Wirta v. Alameda-Contra Costa Transit District*, the court held that where motor coaches were a forum for commercial advertising, refusal to accept a proposed peace message violated the First Amendment guarantee of free speech. It said:

> [Defendants], having opened a forum for the expression of ideas by providing facilities for advertisements on its buses,

cannot for reasons of administrative convenience decline to accept advertisements expressing opinions and beliefs within the ambit [area of influence] of First Amendment protection. . . .

Not only does the district's policy prefer certain classes of protected ideas over others but it goes even further and affords total freedom of the forum to mercantile messages while banning the vast majority of opinions and beliefs extant which enjoy First Amendment protection because of their noncommercialism.

Tinker v. Des Moines Established Students' Right to Free Expression of Ideas

Defendants would have the court find that the school's action is protected because plaintiffs have no right of access to the school newspaper. They argue that the recent Supreme Court case of *Tinker v. Des Moines Independent Community School District*, held only that students have the same rights inside the schoolyard that they have as citizens. Therefore, since citizens as yet have no right of access to the private press, plaintiffs are entitled to no greater privilege.

In *Tinker*, the plaintiffs were suspended from school for wearing black armbands to protest the war in Vietnam. The Court held that the wearing of armbands was closely akin to pure speech and that First Amendment rights, "applied in light of the special characteristics of the school environment, are available to teachers and students." The principle of free speech is not confined to classroom discussion:

> The principal use to which the schools are dedicated is to accommodate students during prescribed hours for the purpose of certain types of activities. Among those activities is personal intercommunication among the students. This is not only an inevitable part of the process of attending school. It is also an important part of the educational process. A student's rights therefore, do not embrace merely the classroom

Young people register with the draft board during the Vietnam War. In Zucker v. Panitz, *the circuit court ruled that the* Huguenot Herald *had already demonstrated that the war was a valid part of its identity as an "educational device" by covering such controversial topics as the war draft board.* © AP Images.

hours. When he is in the cafeteria, or on the playing field, or on the campus during the authorized hours, he may express his opinions, even on controversial subjects like the conflict in Vietnam, if he does so without "materially and substantially [interfering] with the requirement of appropriate discipline in the operation of the school" and without colliding with the rights of others.

Defendants have told the court that the *Huguenot Herald* is not a newspaper in the usual sense, but is part of the curriculum and an educational device. However, it is inconsistent for them to also espouse the position that the school's action is protected because there is no general right of access to the private press.

We have found, from review of its contents, that within the context of the school and educational environment, [the paper] is a forum for the dissemination of ideas. Our problem then, as in *Tinker*, "lies in the area where students in the exercise of First Amendment rights collide with the rules of the school authorities." Here, the school paper appears to have been open to free expression of ideas in the news and editorial columns as well as in letters to the editor. It is patently unfair in light of the free speech doctrine to close to the students the forum which they deem effective to present their ideas. The rationale of *Tinker* carries beyond the facts in that case.

Tinker also disposes of defendants' contention that cases involving advertising in public facilities are inapposite [not relevant] because a school and a school newspaper are not public facilities in the same sense as buses and terminals—that is, they invite only a portion of the public.

This lawsuit arises at a time when many in the educational community oppose the tactics of the young in securing a political voice. It would be both incongruous and dangerous for this court to hold that students who wish to express their views on matters intimately related to them, through traditionally accepted non-disruptive modes of communication, may be precluded from doing so by that same adult community.

Plaintiffs' motion for summary judgment is granted.

> *"A school may refuse to lend its name
> and resources to the dissemination
> of student expression."*

Schools May Censor School-Sponsored Student Publications

The Supreme Court's Decision

Byron White

In the following majority opinion in Hazelwood v. Kuhlmeier, *Supreme Court justice Byron White explains why the principal of Hazelwood East High School censored articles in the school newspaper and concludes that he acted reasonably in doing so. A school newspaper is not a public forum, White declares, and a school need not promote speech inconsistent with its basic educational mission in an activity that is part of the school curriculum. This is a different issue from the one in* Tinker v. Des Moines, *he says, and therefore that precedent does not apply; thus there was no violation of the First Amendment in this case.*

Byron White, Majority opinion, *Hazelwood School District v. Kuhlmeier*, US Supreme Court, January 13, 1988. Copyright © 1988 United States Supreme Court.

The practice at Hazelwood East during the spring 1983 semester was for the journalism teacher [Howard Emerson] to submit page proofs of each *Spectrum* issue to Principal [Robert Eugene] Reynolds for his review prior to publication. On May 10 [1983], Emerson delivered the proofs of the May 13 edition to Reynolds, who objected to two of the articles scheduled to appear in that edition. One of the stories described three Hazelwood East students' experiences with pregnancy; the other discussed the impact of divorce on students at the school.

Reynolds was concerned that, although the pregnancy story used false names "to keep the identity of these girls a secret," the pregnant students still might be identifiable from the text. He also believed that the article's references to sexual activity and birth control were inappropriate for some of the younger students at the school. In addition, Reynolds was concerned that a student identified by name in the divorce story had complained that her father "wasn't spending enough time with my mom, my sister and I" prior to the divorce, "was always out of town on business or out late playing cards with the guys," and "always argued about everything" with her mother. Reynolds believed that the student's parents should have been given an opportunity to respond to these remarks, or to consent to their publication. He was unaware that Emerson had deleted the student's name from the final version of the article.

Reynolds believed that there was no time to make the necessary changes in the stories before the scheduled press run, and that the newspaper would not appear before the end of the school year if printing were delayed to any significant extent. He concluded that his only options under the circumstances were to publish a four-page newspaper instead of the planned six-page newspaper [by] eliminating the two pages on which the offending

---

Image on following page: Robert Reynolds, principal of Hazelwood East High School, stands with a copy of the Spectrum. *The Supreme Court ruled that school officials are justified in censoring school-supported publications.* © AP Images/James A. Finley.

stories appeared, or to publish no newspaper at all. Accordingly, he directed Emerson to withhold from publication the two pages containing the stories on pregnancy and divorce. He informed his superiors of the decision, and they concurred.

District Court and Circuit Court Decisions

Respondents [three former Hazelwood East students who were staff members of *Spectrum*] subsequently commenced this action in the United States District Court for the Eastern District of Missouri [by] seeking a declaration that their First Amendment rights had been violated, injunctive relief, and monetary damages. After a bench trial, the District Court denied an injunction, holding that no First Amendment violation had occurred. . . .

The court found that Principal Reynolds' concern that the pregnant students' anonymity would be lost and their privacy invaded was "legitimate and reasonable," given "the small number of pregnant students at Hazelwood East and several identifying characteristics that were disclosed in the article." The court held that Reynolds' action was also justified "to avoid the impression that [the school] endorses the sexual norms of the subjects" and to shield younger students from exposure to unsuitable material. The deletion of the article on divorce was seen by the court as a reasonable response to the invasion of privacy concerns raised by the named student's remarks. Because the article did not indicate that the student's parents had been offered an opportunity to respond to her allegations, said the court, there was cause for "serious doubt that the article complied with the rules of fairness which are standard in the field of journalism and which were covered in the textbook used in the Journalism II class." Furthermore, the court concluded that Reynolds was justified in deleting two full pages of the newspaper, instead of deleting only the pregnancy and divorce stories or requiring that those stories be modified to address his concerns, based on his "reasonable belief that he had to make an immediate decision and that there was no time to make modifications to the articles in question."

The Court of Appeals for the Eighth Circuit reversed. The court held at the outset that *Spectrum* was not only "a part of the school adopted curriculum," but also a public forum, because the newspaper was "intended to be and operated as a conduit for student viewpoint." The court then concluded that *Spectrum*'s status as a public forum precluded school officials from censoring its contents except when "necessary to avoid material and substantial interference with school work or discipline . . . or the rights of others."

The Court of Appeals found "no evidence in the record that the principal could have reasonably forecast that the censored articles or any materials in the censored articles would have materially disrupted classwork or given rise to substantial disorder in the school."

School officials were entitled to censor the articles on the ground that they invaded the rights of others, according to the court, only if publication of the articles could have resulted in tort liability to [that is, a lawsuit against] the school. The court concluded that no tort action for libel or invasion of privacy could have been maintained against the school by the subjects of the two articles or by their families. Accordingly, the court held that school officials had violated respondents' First Amendment rights by deleting the two pages of the newspaper.

We granted *certiorari* [review], and we now reverse.

Rights of Students in School Are Not the Same as Those of Adults

[As stated in *Tinker v. Des Moines*] Students in the public schools do not "shed their constitutional rights to freedom of speech or expression at the schoolhouse gate." They cannot be punished merely for expressing their personal views on the school premises—whether "in the cafeteria, or on the playing field, or on the campus during the authorized hours,"—unless school authorities

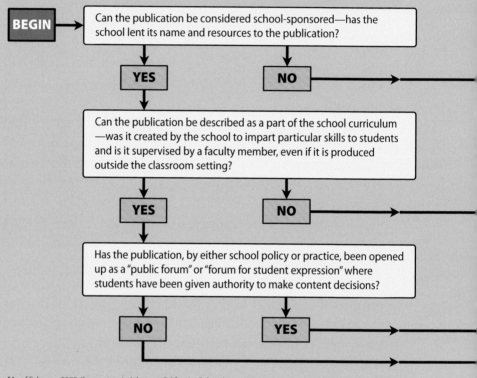

FIRST AMENDMENT RIGHTS OF PUBLIC HIGH SCHOOL STUDENT JOURNALISTS AFTER *HAZELWOOD SCHOOL DISTRICT V. KUHLMEIER*

This diagram describes how a court would determine if a particular act of censorship by school officials is legally permissable.

BEGIN → Can the publication be considered school-sponsored—has the school lent its name and resources to the publication?

YES / **NO** →

Can the publication be described as a part of the school curriculum —was it created by the school to impart particular skills to students and is it supervised by a faculty member, even if it is produced outside the classroom setting?

YES / **NO** →

Has the publication, by either school policy or practice, been opened up as a "public forum" or "forum for student expression" where students have been given authority to make content decisions?

NO / **YES** →

*As of February 2008, if your state is Arkansas, California, Colorado, Iowa, Kansas, Massachusetts, Oregon, Pennsylvania or Washington, the censorship may not be permitted under your state law or regulations.

Taken from: "First Amendment Rights of Public High School Student Journalists After *Hazelwood School District v. Kuhlmeier,*" Student Press Law Center, 2008. www.splc.org.

have reason to believe that such expression will "substantially interfere with the work of the school or impinge upon the rights of other students."

We have nonetheless recognized that the First Amendment rights of students in the public schools "are not automatically coextensive with the rights of adults in other settings," [in] *Bethel*

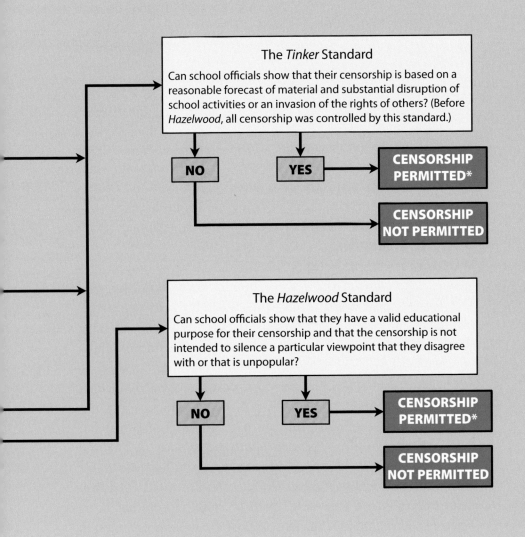

The *Tinker* Standard

Can school officials show that their censorship is based on a reasonable forecast of material and substantial disruption of school activities or an invasion of the rights of others? (Before *Hazelwood*, all censorship was controlled by this standard.)

NO   **YES** → **CENSORSHIP PERMITTED***

CENSORSHIP NOT PERMITTED

The *Hazelwood* Standard

Can school officials show that they have a valid educational purpose for their censorship and that the censorship is not intended to silence a particular viewpoint that they disagree with or that is unpopular?

NO   **YES** → **CENSORSHIP PERMITTED***

CENSORSHIP NOT PERMITTED

School District No. 403 v. Fraser, and must be "applied in light of the special characteristics of the school environment," *Tinker.* A school need not tolerate student speech that is inconsistent with its "basic educational mission," *Fraser,* even though the government could not censor similar speech outside the school. Accordingly, we held in *Fraser* that a student could be disciplined for having delivered a speech that was "sexually explicit" but not legally obscene at an official school assembly, because the school was entitled to "disassociate itself" from the speech in a manner that would demonstrate to others that such vulgarity is "wholly inconsistent with the 'fundamental values' of public school education." We thus recognized that "[t]he determination of what manner of speech in the classroom or in school assembly is inappropriate properly rests with the school board," rather than with the federal courts. It is in this context that respondents' First Amendment claims must be considered.

Was the School Newspaper a Public Forum?

We deal first with the question whether *Spectrum* may appropriately be characterized as a forum for public expression. The public schools do not possess all of the attributes of streets, parks, and other traditional public forums that "time out of mind, have been used for purposes of assembly, communicating thoughts between citizens, and discussing public questions," *Hague v. CIO*. Hence, school facilities may be deemed to be public forums only if school authorities have "by policy or by practice" opened those facilities "for indiscriminate use by the general public," *Perry Education Assn. v. Perry Local Educators' Assn.*, or by some segment of the public, such as student organizations. If the facilities have instead been reserved for other intended purposes, "communicative or otherwise," then no public forum has been created, and school officials may impose reasonable restrictions on the speech of students, teachers, and other members of the school community. . . .

The Hazelwood East Curriculum Guide described the Journalism II course as a "laboratory situation in which the students publish the school newspaper [by] applying skills they have learned in Journalism I." The lessons that were to be learned from the Journalism II course, according to the Curriculum Guide, included development of journalistic skills under deadline pressure, "the legal, moral, and ethical restrictions imposed upon journalists within the school community," and "responsibility and acceptance of criticism for articles of opinion." Journalism II was taught by a faculty member during regular class hours. Students received grades and academic credit for their performance in the course. . . .

The District Court found that Robert Stergos, the journalism teacher during most of the 1982–1983 school year, "both had the authority to exercise, and in fact exercised, a great deal of control over *Spectrum*." For example, Stergos selected the editors of the newspaper, scheduled publication dates, decided the number of pages for each issue, assigned story ideas to class members, advised students on the development of their stories, reviewed the use of quotations, edited stories, selected and edited the letters to the editor, and dealt with the printing company. Many of these decisions were made without consultation with the Journalism II students. The District Court thus found it "clear that Mr. Stergos was the final authority with respect to almost every aspect of the production and publication of *Spectrum*, including its content."

Moreover, after each *Spectrum* issue had been finally approved by Stergos or his successor, the issue still had to be reviewed by Principal Reynolds prior to publication. Respondents' assertion that they had believed that they could publish "practically anything" in *Spectrum* was therefore dismissed by the District Court as simply "not credible." . . .

The evidence relied upon by the Court of Appeals in finding *Spectrum* to be a public forum, is equivocal, at best. . . .

That students were permitted to exercise some authority over the contents of *Spectrum* was fully consistent with the Curriculum Guide objective of teaching the Journalism II students "leadership responsibilities as issue and page editors." A decision to teach leadership skills in the context of a classroom activity hardly implies a decision to relinquish school control over that activity. In sum, the evidence relied upon by the Court of Appeals fails to demonstrate the "clear intent to create a public forum," *Cornelius* [*v. NAACP*], that existed in cases in which we found public forums to have been created. School officials did not evince either "by policy or by practice," *Perry Education Assn.*, any intent to open the pages of *Spectrum* to "indiscriminate use," by its student reporters and editors, or by the student body generally. Instead, they "reserve[d] the forum for its intended purpos[e]," as a supervised learning experience for journalism students. Accordingly, school officials were entitled to regulate the contents of *Spectrum* in any reasonable manner. It is this standard, rather than our decision in *Tinker*, that governs this case.

The Issue in *Tinker* Is Different from the Issue in *Hazelwood*

The question whether the First Amendment requires a school to tolerate particular student Speech—the question that we addressed in *Tinker*—is different from the question whether the First Amendment requires a school affirmatively to promote particular student speech. The former question addresses educators' ability to silence a student's personal expression that happens to occur on the school premises. The latter question concerns educators' authority over school-sponsored publications, theatrical productions, and other expressive activities that students, parents, and members of the public might reasonably perceive to bear the imprimatur of the school. These activities may fairly be characterized as part of the school curriculum, [regardless of] whether . . . they occur in a traditional classroom setting, so long as they are supervised by faculty members and designed to impart particular knowledge or skills to student participants and audiences.

Educators are entitled to exercise greater control over this second form of student expression to assure that participants learn whatever lessons the activity is designed to teach, that readers or listeners are not exposed to material that may be inappropriate for their level of maturity, and that the views of the individual speaker are not erroneously attributed to the school. Hence, a school may, in its capacity as publisher of a school newspaper or producer of a school play, "disassociate itself," *Fraser*, not only from speech that would "substantially interfere with [its] work . . . or impinge upon the rights of other students," *Tinker*, but also from speech that is, for example, ungrammatical, poorly written, inadequately researched, biased or prejudiced, vulgar or profane, or unsuitable for immature audiences. A school must be able to set high standards for the student speech that is disseminated under its auspices—standards that may be higher than those demanded by some newspaper publishers or theatrical producers in the "real" world—and may refuse to disseminate student speech that does not meet those standards. In addition, a school must be able to take into account the emotional maturity of the intended audience in determining whether to disseminate student speech on potentially sensitive topics, which might range from the existence of Santa Claus in an elementary school setting to the particulars of teenage sexual activity in a high school setting. A school must also retain the authority to refuse to sponsor student speech that might reasonably be perceived to advocate drug or alcohol use, irresponsible sex, or conduct otherwise inconsistent with "the shared values of a civilized social order," *Fraser*, or to associate the school with any position other than neutrality on matters of political controversy. Otherwise, the schools would be unduly constrained from fulfilling their role as "a principal instrument in awakening the child to cultural values, in preparing him for later professional training, and in helping him to adjust normally to his environment," *Brown v. Board of Education*.

Accordingly, we conclude that the standard articulated in *Tinker* for determining when a school may punish student expression need not also be the standard for determining when a school may refuse to lend its name and resources to the dissemination of student expression. Instead, we hold that educators do not offend the First Amendment by exercising editorial control over the style and content of student speech in school-sponsored expressive activities, so long as their actions are reasonably related to legitimate pedagogical concerns.

This standard is consistent with our oft-expressed view that the education of the Nation's youth is primarily the responsibility of parents, teachers, and state and local school officials, and not of federal judges. It is only when the decision to censor a school-sponsored publication, theatrical production, or other vehicle of student expression has no valid educational purpose that the First Amendment is so "directly and sharply implicate[d]" as to require judicial intervention to protect students' constitutional rights.

The Principal Acted Reasonably

We also conclude that Principal Reynolds acted reasonably in requiring the deletion from the May 13 [1983] issue of *Spectrum* of the pregnancy article, the divorce article, and the remaining articles that were to appear on the same pages of the newspaper.

The initial paragraph of the pregnancy article declared that "[a]ll names have been changed to keep the identity of these girls a secret." The principal concluded that the students' anonymity was not adequately protected, however, given the other identifying information in the article and the small number of pregnant students at the school. Indeed, a teacher at the school credibly testified that she could positively identify at least one of the girls, and possibly all three. It is likely that many students at Hazelwood East would have been at least as successful in identifying the girls. Reynolds therefore could reasonably have feared that the article violated whatever pledge of anonymity had been given to the pregnant students. In addition, he could reasonably have been concerned that the article was not sufficiently sensitive to the privacy interests of the students' boyfriends and parents, who were discussed in the article but who were given no opportunity to consent to its publication or to offer a response. The article did not contain graphic accounts of sexual activity. The girls did comment in the article, however, concerning their sexual histories and their use or nonuse of birth control. It was not unreasonable for the principal to have concluded that such frank talk was inappropriate in a school-sponsored publication distributed to 14-year-old freshmen and presumably taken home to be read by students' even younger brothers and sisters.

The student who was quoted by name in the version of the divorce article seen by Principal Reynolds made comments sharply critical of her father. The principal could reasonably have concluded that an individual publicly identified as an inattentive parent—indeed, as one who chose "playing cards with the guys" over home and family—was entitled to an opportunity to defend himself as a matter of journalistic fairness. These concerns were shared by both of *Spectrum*'s faculty advisers for the 1982–1983 school year, who testified that they would not have allowed the article to be printed without deletion of the student's name.

Principal Reynolds testified credibly at trial that, at the time that he reviewed the proofs of the May 13 [1983] issue during an extended telephone conversation with Emerson, he believed that there was no time to make any changes in the articles, and that the newspaper had to be printed immediately or not at all. . . .

Reynolds could reasonably have concluded that the students who had written and edited these articles had not sufficiently mastered those portions of the Journalism II curriculum that pertained to the treatment of controversial issues and personal attacks, the need to protect the privacy of individuals whose most intimate concerns are to be revealed in the newspaper, and "the legal, moral, and ethical restrictions imposed upon journalists within [a] school community" that includes adolescent subjects and readers. Finally, we conclude that the principal's decision to delete two pages of *Spectrum*, rather than to delete only the offending articles or to require that they be modified, was reasonable under the circumstances as he understood them. Accordingly, no violation of First Amendment rights occurred.

The judgment of the Court of Appeals for the Eighth Circuit is therefore *reversed.*

> "The case before us aptly illustrates
> how readily school officials . . . can
> camouflage viewpoint discrimination
> as the 'mere' protection of students."

No Distinction Should Be Made Between Personal and School-Sponsored Publications

Dissenting Opinion

William J. Brennan

In the following dissenting opinion in Hazelwood v. Kuhlmeier, *Supreme Court Justice William J. Brennan expresses his disagreement with the Court's majority decision that censorship of school-sponsored projects such as school newspapers is permissible even though it is a violation of the First Amendment to suppress other student expression. He does not believe there are grounds for making such a distinction. He claims the one thing that might justify it—the risk that views expressed in the newspaper might be attributed to the school—could be dealt with by other means, such as publication of a disclaimer. Furthermore, he maintains the principal of Hazelwood East High School accomplished the censorship*

William J. Brennan, Dissenting opinion, *Hazelwood School District v. Kuhlmeier*, US Supreme Court, January 13, 1988. Copyright © 1988 United States Supreme Court.

in an arbitrary manner, and the Court's ruling will therefore teach young people the wrong kind of civics lesson.

When the young men and women of Hazelwood East High School registered for Journalism II, they expected a civics lesson. *Spectrum*, the newspaper they were to publish, "was not just a class exercise in which students learned to prepare papers and hone writing skills, it was a . . . forum established to give students an opportunity to express their views while gaining an appreciation of their rights and responsibilities under the First Amendment to the United States Constitution. . . ."

The school board itself affirmatively guaranteed the students of Journalism II an atmosphere conducive to fostering such an appreciation and exercising the full panoply of rights associated with a free student press. "School-sponsored student publications," it vowed, "will not restrict free expression or diverse viewpoints within the rules of responsible journalism."

This case arose when the Hazelwood East administration breached its own promise, dashing its students' expectations. The school principal, without prior consultation or explanation, excised six articles—comprising two full pages—of the May 13, 1983, issue of *Spectrum*. He did so not because any of the articles would "materially and substantially interfere with the requirements of appropriate discipline," but simply because he considered two of the six "inappropriate, personal, sensitive, and unsuitable" for student consumption.

Educators Must Allow Some Student Expression that Offends Them

In my view, the principal broke more than just a promise. He violated the First Amendment's prohibitions against censorship of any student expression that neither disrupts classwork nor invades the rights of others, and against any censorship that is not narrowly tailored to serve its purpose. . . .

A dissent to the Hazelwood *ruling stated that the motive for censoring the work of student journalists like these in Summit, Missouri, cannot be considered educational when administrators are concerned for the audience or the school itself rather than the student journalist.* © AP Images/Orlin Wagner.

While the "constitutional rights of students in public school are not automatically coextensive with the rights of adults in other settings," *Fraser*, students in the public schools do not "shed their constitutional rights to freedom of speech or expression at the schoolhouse gate," *Tinker*. Just as the public on the street corner must, in the interest of fostering "enlightened opinion," *Cantwell v. Connecticut*, tolerate speech that "tempt[s] [the listener] to throw [the speaker] off the street," public educators must accommodate some student expression even if it offends them or offers views or values that contradict those the school wishes to inculcate.

In *Tinker*, this Court struck the balance. We held that official censorship of student expression—there the suspension of several students until they removed their armbands protesting the Vietnam war—is unconstitutional unless the speech "materially disrupts classwork or involves substantial disorder or invasion of the rights of others." School officials may not suppress "silent, passive expression of opinion, unaccompanied by any disorder or disturbance on the part of" the speaker. The "mere desire to avoid the discomfort and unpleasantness that always accompany an unpopular viewpoint," or an unsavory subject, does not justify official suppression of student speech in the high school.

This Court applied the *Tinker* test just a Term ago in *Fraser*, upholding an official decision to discipline a student for delivering a lewd speech in support of a student government candidate. The Court today casts no doubt on *Tinker's* vitality. Instead, it erects a taxonomy of school censorship, concluding that *Tinker* applies to one category, and not another. On the one hand is censorship "to silence a student's personal expression that happens to occur on the school premises." On the other hand is censorship of expression that arises in the context of "school-sponsored . . . expressive activities that students, parents, and members of the public might reasonably perceive to bear the imprimatur of the school."

The Court does not, for it cannot, purport to discern from our precedents the distinction it creates. One could, I suppose, readily characterize the students' symbolic speech in *Tinker* as "personal expression that happens to [have] occur[red] on school premises," although *Tinker* did not even hint that the personal nature of the speech was of any (much less dispositive [evidence-related]) relevance. But that same description could not, by any stretch of the imagination, fit Fraser's speech. He did not just "happen" to deliver his lewd speech to an *ad hoc* [impromptu] gathering on the playground. As the second paragraph of *Fraser* evinces, if ever a forum for student expression was "school-sponsored," Fraser's was:

Fraser . . . delivered a speech nominating a fellow student for student elective office. Approximately 600 high school students . . . attended the assembly. Students were required to attend the assembly or to report to the study hall. The assembly was part of a *school-sponsored* educational program in self-government.

Yet, from the first sentence of its analysis, *Fraser* faithfully applied *Tinker*.

Nor has this Court ever intimated a distinction between personal and school-sponsored speech in any other context. . . .

The Excuses Do Not Support Distinction Between School-Sponsored and Other Speech

Even if we were writing on a clean slate, I would reject the Court's rationale for abandoning *Tinker* in this case. The Court offers no more than an obscure tangle of three excuses to afford educators "greater control" over school-sponsored speech than the *Tinker* test would permit: the public educator's prerogative to control curriculum; the pedagogical interest in shielding the high school audience from objectionable viewpoints and sensitive topics; and the school's need to dissociate itself from student expression. None of the excuses, once disentangled, supports the distinction that the Court draws. *Tinker* fully addresses the first concern; the second is illegitimate; and the third is readily achievable through less oppressive means.

The Court is certainly correct that the First Amendment permits educators "to assure that participants learn whatever lessons the activity is designed to teach. . . ." That is, however, the essence of the *Tinker* test, not an excuse to abandon it. Under *Tinker*, school officials may censor only such student speech as would "materially disrup[t]" a legitimate curricular function. Manifestly, student speech is more likely to disrupt a curricular function when it arises in the context of a curricular activity— one that "is designed to teach" something—than when it arises in the context of a noncurricular activity. Thus, under *Tinker*, the school may constitutionally punish the budding political orator if he disrupts calculus class, but not if he holds his tongue for the cafeteria. That is not because some more stringent standard applies in the curricular context. (After all, this Court applied the same standard whether the students in *Tinker* wore their armbands to the "classroom" or the "cafeteria." It is because student speech in the noncurricular context is less likely to disrupt materially any legitimate pedagogical purpose.

I fully agree with the Court that the First Amendment should afford an educator the prerogative not to sponsor the publication of a newspaper article that is "ungrammatical, poorly written, inadequately researched, biased or prejudiced," or that falls short of the "high standards for . . . student speech that is disseminated under [the school's] auspices. . . ." But we need not abandon *Tinker* to reach that conclusion; we need only apply it. The enumerated criteria reflect the skills that the curricular newspaper "is designed to teach." The educator may, under *Tinker*, constitutionally "censor" poor grammar, writing, or research, because to reward such expression would "materially disrup[t]" the newspaper's curricular purpose.

The same cannot be said of official censorship designed to shield the *audience* or dissociate the *sponsor* from the expression. Censorship so motivated might well serve (although, as I demonstrate, cannot legitimately serve) some other school purpose. But it in no way furthers the curricular purposes of a student *newspaper* unless one believes that the purpose of the school newspaper is to teach students that the press ought never report bad news, express unpopular views, or print a thought that might upset its sponsors. Unsurprisingly, Hazelwood East claims no such pedagogical purpose.

The Principal's Action Was Not a Lesson in Journalism

The Court relies on bits of testimony to portray the principal's conduct as a pedagogical lesson to Journalism II students who "had not sufficiently mastered those portions of the . . . curriculum that pertained to the treatment of controversial issues and personal attacks, the need to protect the privacy of individuals . . . and the 'legal, moral, and ethical restrictions imposed upon journalists. . . .'"

But the principal never consulted the students before censoring their work. "[T]hey learned of the deletions when the paper was released. . . ." Further, he explained the deletions only in the broadest of generalities. In one meeting called at the behest of seven protesting *Spectrum* staff members (presumably a fraction of the full class), he characterized the articles as "'too sensitive' for 'our immature audience of readers,'" and in a later meeting he deemed them simply "inappropriate, personal, sensitive and unsuitable for the newspaper." The Court's supposition that the principal intended (or the protesters understood) those generalities as a lesson on the nuances of journalistic responsibility is utterly incredible. If he did, a fact that neither the District Court nor the Court of Appeals found, the lesson was lost on all but the psychic *Spectrum* staffer.

The Court's second excuse for deviating from precedent is the school's interest in shielding an impressionable high school audience from material whose substance is "unsuitable for immature audiences." . . .

Tinker teaches us that the state educator's undeniable, and undeniably vital, mandate to inculcate moral and political values is not a general warrant to act as "thought police" stifling discussion of all but state-approved topics and advocacy of all but the official position. Otherwise, educators could transform students into "closed-circuit recipients of only that which the State chooses to communicate," *Tinker*, and cast a perverse and impermissible "pall of orthodoxy over the classroom," *Keyishian v. Board of Regents*. Thus, the State cannot constitutionally prohibit its high school students from recounting in the locker room "the particulars of [their] teen-age sexual activity," nor even from advocating "irresponsible se[x]" or other presumed abominations of "the shared values of a civilized social order." Even in its capacity as educator, the State may not assume an Orwellian [destructive to a free society] "guardianship of the public mind," *Thomas v. Collins*.

School Sponsorship Does Not Justify Thought Control

The mere fact of school sponsorship does not, as the Court suggests, license such thought control in the high school, whether through school suppression of disfavored viewpoints or through official assessment of topic sensitivity. The former would constitute unabashed and unconstitutional viewpoint discrimination, as well as an impermissible infringement of the students' "right to receive information and ideas." Just as a school board may not purge its state-funded library of all books that "offen[d] [its] social, political and moral tastes," school officials may not, out of like motivation, discriminatorily excise objectionable ideas from a student publication. The State's prerogative to dissolve the student newspaper entirely (or to limit its subject matter) no more entitles it to dictate which viewpoints students may express on its pages than the State's prerogative to close down the schoolhouse entitles it to prohibit the nondisruptive expression of antiwar sentiment within its gates.

Official censorship of student speech on the ground that it addresses "potentially sensitive topics" is, for related reasons, equally impermissible. I would not begrudge an educator the authority to limit the substantive scope of a school-sponsored publication to a certain, objectively definable topic, such as literary criticism, school sports, or an overview of the school year. Unlike those determinate limitations, "potential topic sensitivity" is a vaporous nonstandard. . . .

The case before us aptly illustrates how readily school officials (and courts) can camouflage viewpoint discrimination as the "mere" protection of students from sensitive topics. Among the grounds that the Court advances to uphold the principal's censorship of one of the articles was the potential sensitivity of "teenage sexual activity." Yet the District Court specifically found that the principal "did not, as a matter of principle, oppose discussion of said topi[c] in *Spectrum*." That much is also clear from the same principal's approval of the "squeal law" article on the same page, dealing forthrightly with "teenage sexuality," "the use of contraceptives by teenagers," and "teenage pregnancy." If topic sensitivity were the true basis of the principal's decision, the two articles should have been equally objectionable. It is much more likely that the objectionable article was objectionable because of the viewpoint it expressed: it might have been read (as the majority apparently does) to advocate "irresponsible sex."

The School Could Disclaim Ideas Without Censorship

The sole concomitant of school sponsorship that might conceivably justify the distinction that the Court draws between sponsored and nonsponsored student expression is the risk "that the views of the individual speaker [might be] erroneously attributed to the school." Of course, the risk of erroneous attribution inheres in any student expression, including "personal expression" that, like the armbands in *Tinker*, "happens to occur on the school premises." Nevertheless, the majority is certainly correct that indicia [indications] of school sponsorship increase the likelihood of such attribution, and that state educators may therefore have a legitimate interest in dissociating themselves from student speech.

But "[e]ven though the governmental purpose be legitimate and substantial, that purpose cannot be pursued by means that broadly stifle fundamental personal liberties when the end can be more narrowly achieved," *Keyishian v. Board of Regents*. Dissociative means short of censorship are available to the school. It could, for example, require the student activity to publish a disclaimer, such as the "Statement of Policy" that *Spectrum* published each school year announcing that "[a]ll . . . editorials appearing in this newspaper reflect the opinions of the *Spectrum* staff, which are not necessarily shared by the administrators or faculty of Hazelwood East"; or it could simply issue its own response clarifying the official position on the matter and explaining why the student position is wrong. Yet, without so much as acknowledging the less oppressive alternatives, the Court approves of brutal censorship.

Since the censorship served no legitimate pedagogical purpose, it cannot by any stretch of the imagination have been designed to prevent "materia[l] disrupt[tion of] classwork," *Tinker*. Nor did the censorship fall within the category that *Tinker* described as necessary to prevent student expression from "inva[ding] the rights of others." If that term is to have any content, it must be limited to rights that are protected by law. "Any yardstick less exacting than [that] could result in school officials curtailing speech at the slightest fear of disturbance," a prospect that would be completely at odds with this Court's pronouncement that the undifferentiated fear or apprehension of disturbance is not enough [even in the public school context] to overcome the right to freedom of expression. *Tinker*. And, as the Court of Appeals correctly reasoned, whatever journalistic impropriety these articles may have contained, they could not conceivably be tortious [cause for suit], much less criminal.

Finally, even if the majority were correct that the principal could constitutionally have censored the objectionable material, I would emphatically object to the brutal manner in which he did so. Where "[t]he separation of legitimate from illegitimate speech calls for more sensitive tools," *Speiser v. Randall*, the principal used a paper shredder. He objected to some material in two articles, but excised six entire articles. He did not so much as inquire into obvious alternatives, such as precise deletions or additions (one of which had already been made), rearranging the layout, or delaying publication. Such unthinking contempt for individual rights is intolerable from any state official. It is particularly insidious from one to whom the public entrusts the task of inculcating in its youth an appreciation for the cherished democratic liberties that our Constitution guarantees.

The Court opens its analysis in this case by purporting to reaffirm *Tinker's* time-tested proposition that public school students "do not 'shed their constitutional rights to freedom of speech or expression at the schoolhouse gate.'" (quoting *Tinker*). That is an ironic introduction to an opinion that denudes high school students of much of the First Amendment protection that *Tinker* itself prescribed. Instead of "teach[ing] children to respect the diversity of ideas that is fundamental to the American system," *Board of Education v. Pico*, and "that our Constitution is a living reality, not parchment preserved under glass," *Shanley v. Northeast Independent School Dist., Bexar Cty., Tex.*, the Court today "teach[es] youth to discount important principles of our government as mere platitudes." *West Virginia Board of Education v. Barnette*. The young men and women of Hazelwood East expected a civics lesson, but not the one the Court teaches them today.

> *"Even schools that have allowed student editors to make their own content decisions for the print version of a student newspaper have censored an online edition."*

The *Hazelwood* Decision Caused an Increase in Censorship of School Newspapers

Mark Goodman

In the following viewpoint attorney Mark Goodman points out that after the Supreme Court decision in Hazelwood v. Kuhlmeier, *which allowed schools to censor school newspapers, censorship has increased significantly. Many school officials, he says, are more interested in making sure that the school is portrayed favorably to the public than in teaching students the principles of good journalism. Media advisers who refuse to censor are being threatened with the loss of their jobs. Online newspapers are being censored even more than print publications because of their larger potential audience. Some students and teachers are going public with their censorship problems by contacting local media, but too often professional journalists fail to support them. Mark Goodman was the executive director of the Student Press Law Center in Arlington, Virginia, from 1985 to 2007. He is now a professor and the Knight Chair in Scholastic Journalism at Kent State University in Kent, Ohio.*

For most high school journalism teachers and publication advisers, teaching students to be responsible journalists means instilling in them an unwavering commitment to the public's right to know the truth. In this time of moral ambiguity, that is a surprisingly easy sell to young people, who desperately want to believe their lives can make a difference.

But teaching this lesson, which is at the very heart of the profession of journalism, has never been more difficult. The censorship faced by teen journalists and those who work with them today is constant and debilitating. The consequences, for the future of high school journalism and the entire profession, could be devastating.

Many who have not read a high school newspaper in several decades may be surprised to learn how the medium has grown up. In 1969, the Supreme Court ruled that students had the right to wear black armbands to school to protest the Vietnam War. Students, the Court ruled, do not shed their First Amendment rights at the schoolhouse gate. As a result, public school officials were forced to recognize that some free press protections applied to the high school media. By the early 1980s, courts across the country had ruled that unless public school officials could demonstrate some evidence that substantial disruption of school activities was imminent, they could not censor school-sponsored student publications simply because they were controversial or expressed unpopular views. As a result of these protections, the quality of high school journalism soared as students began to discuss real issues such as teen pregnancy and school board policies instead of limiting their coverage to movie reviews and sports scores.

The Effect of *Hazelwood v. Kuhlmeier*

In January 1988, the Supreme Court pulled the rug out from under the burgeoning success of the high school press. In a case that arose from a school in suburban St. Louis, Missouri, the Court said that school officials had the authority to censor stories about teen pregnancy and divorce from a high school newspaper. In its ruling in *Hazelwood School District v. Kuhlmeier*, the Court said school officials have the authority to censor most avenues of school-sponsored student expression when they can show that their censorship is "reasonably related to legitimate pedagogical concerns." That phrase (Supreme Court legalese for having an educational excuse) dramatically lowered the First Amendment hurdle that lower courts had said school officials had to overcome before they could legally censor student media.

To no one's surprise, requests for legal assistance received by the Student Press Law Center (SPLC) in the years since the ruling have increased dramatically. In 1988, the SPLC received 548 calls for help from students and their advisers around the country. By 1999, that number had increased to more than 1,600.

The sad fact is that for many school officials, their primary commitment is not to teaching students the values of a democratic society or the principles of good journalism but to ensure that their school is portrayed in a positive light, no matter how unrealistic that portrayal may be. Censorship of the student media is one way they achieve that, as dozens of students and advisers tell the Student Press Law Center each month. Some examples:

In Indiana, a principal censored a story that painstakingly described how freshman football players were threatened and beaten by upperclassmen as part of an annual hazing ritual. After the newspaper staff threatened to go to the local media, the principal allowed an edited version of the story to be published.

In California, high school administrators censored a story about the growing popularity of "backyard wrestling," an organized effort by students to mimic television's professional wrestling matches, which sometimes results in physical injuries. Several months later, national news magazines were publishing stories about the phenomenon.

After a Florida student wrote a column criticizing the rap music industry for the role models it creates, her school principal prohibited her from writing any more articles for the newspaper because of her racial insensitivity despite the fact that she never mentioned race in her column.

At a California high school, the principal censored a story about the school's teen parenting program because it would send the wrong message to the community. A neighboring high school newspaper agreed to publish the censored story.

After a Washington State student newspaper published a commentary criticizing the food in the school cafeteria, the principal prohibited the publication of anything "that is critical or might be perceived as critical" of any school staff member or program.

Students are not the only ones who are confronting this censorship. Increasingly school officials are threatening media advisers who refuse to censor their students as the administration demands. Thus advisers dedicated to strong and independent journalism may well find themselves confronted with the choice of protecting their students or saving their [jobs]. It's no surprise that the turnover rate among publication advisers is alarmingly high. Those who stay to fight for their students are true heroes.

Problems in Using the Internet

Perhaps one of the biggest challenges to face the student media in recent years has revolved around changing technology. Teen reporters and editors, like their professional counterparts, have found the Internet an invaluable tool in researching stories and contacting resources. But the growing prevalence of filters on school computers has significantly limited its usefulness. Students and advisers report being blocked from sites dealing with topics like breast cancer and Bosnian war crimes because the school's imprecise filtering software excluded them. After one publication staff found that its school's filters blocked access to the Student

Press Law Center's Web site, they persuaded school officials to provide them an unfiltered computer in their newsroom. Most students are not so lucky.

Moving into online publishing has also caused conflicts. Even schools that have allowed student editors to make their own content decisions for the print version of a student newspaper have censored an online edition or prohibited the publication from creating one altogether. The potential audience available on the World Wide Web makes some school administrators even more concerned about stories that could tarnish the school's image.

Efforts to Fight Censorship

Facing all of these threats and constraints, journalism educators are left to ask themselves whether we are really preparing students for their role as citizen defenders of press freedom. Or is the constant barrage of censorship teaching young people that there is nothing wrong with allowing government officials to dictate what is and is not news and that free expression is to be tolerated only as long as those in authority agree with it?

Despite increasing efforts to silence the student press, many students and teachers make their best effort to fight back. Many go public with their censorship battles, contacting the local media, in order to force school officials to publicly defend their efforts to silence student expression. Some students turn to their own independent means of publishing, through "underground" newspapers produced on a home computer and duplicated at the local copy shop or through an independent Web site. The courts have made it clear that school officials' ability to censor student publications distributed on school grounds that are not school sponsored is much more limited. And for publications created and distributed outside of school (independent Web sites, for example), school officials' ability to punish or censor student expression should be virtually nonexistent. Parents, not schools, have the right to oversee student expression when it occurs outside the boundaries of the school day.

HIGH SCHOOL STUDENT ATTITUDES TOWARD CENSORSHIP OF SCHOOL NEWSPAPERS

High school students should be allowed to report controversial issues in their student newspaper without the approval of school authorities.

	2004	2006	2007
Strongly agree	30%	34%	30%
Mildly agree	28%	30%	28%
Mildly disagree	18%	17%	18%
Strongly disagree	11%	8%	9%
Don't know	13%	11%	14%

Taken from: *The Future of the First Amendment III*, John S. and James L. Knight Foundation, 2007, Appendix A, Question 21. www.firstamendmentfuture.org.

These off-campus forms of expression are an important alternative for censored student journalists. But when press freedom is available only to those students who have the financial means to support it, the voices of poorer rural and urban students are lost. And the benefits of a trained faculty adviser who can teach journalistic skills, ethics and responsibility are missed when students are forced to turn away from school-sponsored media. Youth pages of community newspapers or citywide teen publications supervised by professional editors are a great training ground. But they can seldom reach the same number of students that would be involved in school-sponsored publications at each school.

Censorship of school newspapers has increased since the Hazelwood *decision. The student editors and reporters of the Stow High School newspaper refused to publish an edition of the paper in which administrators had censored the photo of a suicide victim.* © AP Images/ Akron Beacon Journal, Phil Masturzo.

Although the Supreme Court appears to have forsaken high school journalists, some legal protection against censorship remains. The most surprising response to the *Hazelwood* decision and the censorship it has inspired has been the effort to enact state laws giving students free press protections. The Supreme Court's ruling only dictated the limits of First Amendment protections; it left open the possibility that states could create their own laws or regulations that provide student journalists with greater rights than this high court recognized under the federal Constitution. A total of 29 state legislatures have debated such laws, and seven now have them on the books. California, Massachusetts, Iowa, Kansas, Colorado, Oregon and Arkansas have returned high school journalism to the place it was before 1988, saying students will be allowed to express themselves freely in school unless school officials can demonstrate their expression is libelous, obscene or will create a substantial disruption of school activities.

Little Support from Professional Media

One of the most frustrating aspects of this ongoing battle for many students and teachers has been how little support they sometimes receive from the local "professional" media. Most community newspapers and television stations have no idea if the high school media in their community are being censored simply because they have never asked the students who produce them or advisers who work with them.

A high school teacher's job was threatened several years ago because of a controversial feature published in the student yearbook on which she was adviser. "Why are they [the local media] so anxious to see us fail, highlighting what they perceive are our students' mistakes and never willing to defend our right to be less than perfect?" she asked. "Would they really like to be held to the same standard?"

She expressed a sentiment that discussions with student editors and advisers around the country suggest is sharply increasing. A growing number believe that the commercial media are only interested in the First Amendment and press freedom when their rights are being threatened and have little concern about those same rights as they apply to others, especially young people. After 22 years at the Student Press Law Center, I know that [such a] perception is not an accurate reflection of the attitudes of thousands of working reporters and editors at large and small news organizations throughout the nation. But I also know that most of these students will not make journalism their profession and thus will never set foot in a professional newsroom. Their attitudes about and the importance we place on press freedom will be fundamentally shaped by experiences that end the day they graduate from high school.

If we care about the future of journalism, we have to show student journalists that we care about them, too. Professionals who fail to defend student press freedom will have only them-selves to blame when young journalists they hire are one day as indifferent to the First Amendment as many working journalists are now to the problems confronted by the high school press.

| "Only when student journalists write
for an organization independent from
the school [do] they truly get to write
without a censoring administration."

Student Journalists Are Going Online to Avoid Censorship

Jin Moon

In the following article from the Freedom Forum, a nonpartisan foundation that champions the First Amendment as a cornerstone of democracy, Jin Moon writes that many high school students are now publishing independently on the Internet rather than in school newspapers. He explains that when they do this through a news site or on their own, they can deal with controversial subjects that school administrators would censor. Online editions of school newspapers, on the other hand, are subject to approval by school authorities and sometimes have even greater restrictions than print publications.

From publishing independently to posting stories on online student news services, high school students across the country are turning increasingly to the Web to publish articles important to them and to gain freedom from censorship-prone school administrators.

This is more than a trend among young people for whom computers are a way of life.

It's a way of getting out from under the shackles created in 1988 in the form the U.S. Supreme Court's decision in *Hazelwood School District v. Kuhlmeier*. Student journalists, and many of their advisers and journalism organizations across the country, claim the decision creates the opportunity for principals to suppress legitimate publication by public high school students.

Enter the Internet.

With the Internet's growing popularity, especially among young people, and the students' publication problems, it is no surprise that many teens have begun publishing articles on the Web.

News Services for Student Journalists

And [those teens] are getting help from online news services that have blossomed amid the growing popularity of student Web journalism.

Monette Austin Bailey, editor in chief of Children's Express Worldwide News Service online, said her news site provides young journalists with an alternative to the school newspaper, which in most states falls subject to *Hazelwood* (six states have afforded student journalists greater freedom than does *Hazelwood*). Children's Express is an international news service, reported and edited by young people from 8 to 18 for adult print, broadcast and online media. Children's Express articles are carried by newspapers across the country and are included on the *New York Times* News Service.

Bailey said her news site allows young reporters to write about controversial topics that are pertinent to the average teenager.

"Many of our kids have said they like working for Children's Express because we allow them to do what interests them, not what the adults are interested in," she said. "They are able to pursue a story on, say, date rape, without being worried that we'll kill the idea before it even gets to the interviewing stage. We do warn them that our subscribers may not run the story, but that doesn't mean we won't try.

"Kids come to Children's Express for leadership and journalism opportunities they may not get in a school setting," Bailey said. "We treat them like the adults we want them to become. We explain consequences and libel and free speech and then guide them in the best way to handle all of that."

Student reporters often come to the Children's Express newsroom after school a couple of times a week.

In the Washington, D.C., bureau of Children's Express, Ayesha Johnson, 16, said she doesn't write for her school newspaper because the experience would be too limiting.

"You can't really talk in-depth about stuff like abortion . . . because the paper doesn't want to offend anyone," said Johnson, who attends Ballou High School in Washington, D.C. Johnson joined Children's Express a year ago [in 1999], and said her experience thus far had made her a better journalist than she would have been as a reporter for her school newspaper.

"I get to do a lot of field work," she said. "I get to go out and just do it."

Johnson said she believes that if *Hazelwood* were overturned, it would be beneficial to student journalists.

"I absolutely see the principals' point of view, but they're like overprotective parents," she said. "Student journalists should have more freedom to make mistakes. . . . As long as [student] journalists keep social responsibility, then I think Hazelwood should be lifted."

More Censorship at Private Schools

The argument for free speech for student journalists is even more difficult at private schools, where administrators have even greater latitude to control it. Since private schools are not restricted by the First Amendment, they can set any guidelines they wish on school publications. Students there, as well, are turning to the Web. They may publish online stories that normally could be excluded from their school's publication, said Mark Goodman, executive director of the Student Press Law Center in Washington, D.C.

"There is a big distinction between school-sponsored publications and student expression outside of school," Goodman said. "If students publish Web sites from their own computers and call the principal names on the Web site, the school cannot censor or punish them for what they publish on the sites."

Matthew Shopsin, a 16-year-old private school student, started writing for the New York bureau of Children's Express at age 9. His older brother wrote for the site and introduced him to the news service. Shopsin's stories have been posted on *The New York Post*'s Web site and been carried by the *Amsterdam News*, also in New York.

Shopsin, who attends the Packer Collegiate Institute in Brooklyn, said he hadn't written for his high school paper yet, but would do so in the future. He says one of the major reasons he hasn't joined the school paper is that it doesn't often take interesting or unusual angles [on] stories.

Shopsin said his school this year passed a Press Rights Amendment Act, which liberates the school newspaper from direct censorship of the administration. The amendment states that the paper would be reviewed only once by the adviser before publication.

However, he says, this policy doesn't help if the adviser is afraid of publishing stories that might offend the administration.

Shopsin says he believes the reasoning behind *Hazelwood* is good in general, but "it makes administrators able to keep anything they want out [of the paper]."

Publishing on the Web

In addition to news services, many young people are striking out on their own—virtually cost-free, but with help. Many Web sites, such as NBCi's Xoom.com and Yahoo's GeoCities.com, offer free Web page space.

Many students publish school-related news and materials online to bypass the censorship of their school newspapers. © AP Images/Mel Evans.

Many high school newspapers already are online as seen on the National Scholastic Press Association's Web site.

About 10,000 high schools across the country use HighWired .com to put their newspapers on the Web, said Glen Mohr, product manager for journalism and guidance at HighWired.com. HighWired.com is the largest network of online school newspapers, and its service is free, fast and easy to get up and running, Mohr said.

Schools who want to use HighWired.com to publish on the Internet must have a faculty adviser to sign a user agreement. The adviser is then given a password to be used when stories are posted. The adviser can give the password to whomever he or she pleases, and HighWired.com will not interfere.

But because most high schools simply post their print edition directly online, the papers have already been filtered through the administration. Thus, it's not exactly censor-free. It is only when student journalists write for an organization independent from the school, such as the Children's Express, that they truly get to write without a censoring administration. (Of course, many

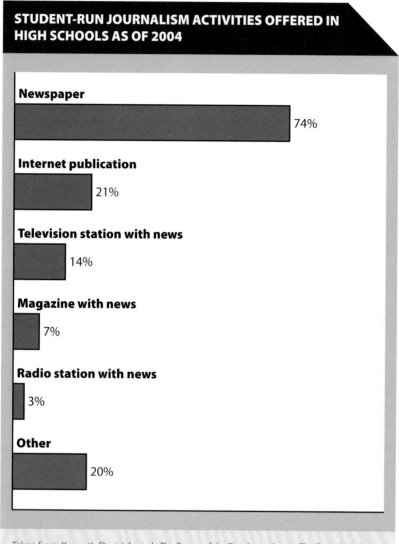

STUDENT-RUN JOURNALISM ACTIVITIES OFFERED IN HIGH SCHOOLS AS OF 2004

Newspaper
74%

Internet publication
21%

Television station with news
14%

Magazine with news
7%

Radio station with news
3%

Other
20%

Taken from: Kenneth Dautrich et al., *The Future of the First Amendment: The Digital Media, Civic Education, and Free Expression Rights in America's High Schools*, Rowman and Littlefield, 2008, p. 37.

schools also have Net-filtering software that keeps students from accessing controversial material from school computers.)

"Most high school newspapers use HighWired.com as a means to put their print edition online," Mohr said. "This means that the same issues regarding student-press rights that arise with print versions also arise with online newspapers [on HighWired .com]."

Mohr also said some administrators have chosen to place greater restrictions on online publications than on print, although the courts have not yet passed a legal distinction between publishing online and publishing in print. Often, school administrators will opt to delete full student names and photos on the Internet, claiming to be protecting student interests.

Valerie Amster, a former journalism teacher who advised the newspaper, yearbook, literary magazine and news bureau at Hampshire High School in Illinois for four years, said she had experienced Web censorship. She currently lives in Richmond, Va., and will be teaching in Henrico County, Va., schools next year.

"Our district technology people [in Hampshire] informed me that if I were to put the paper online, I would have to eliminate pictures and last names," Amster said. "I decided that wasn't actually journalism and since my hands were quite full with the four publications, I didn't pursue it. If I were to stay longer, I would be looking at something like HighWired.com to get my kids' paper online."

Mohr said, "HighWired.com believes that such restrictions deprive students of the opportunity to be recognized for their work. In fact, one of the great advantages schools gain by joining the HighWired.com network is the opportunity for their students' work to be picked up by such major professional media as the *New York Times*, the *Boston Globe*, the *Miami Herald* and many others."

Balancing Freedom and Responsibility

Even online, however, questions continue to arise about how to achieve the delicate balance between journalistic freedom and responsibility.

Mohr believes that restricting student-press freedom online diminishes the educational experience of journalistic work, imposing decisions upon students rather than educating them to make such decisions for themselves.

But Marsha Kalkowski, a journalism teacher and newspaper adviser at Marion High School, a private, all-girls school in Omaha, [Nebraska], believes that because students don't know as much about journalism as professionals, they need guidance from an adult who does know the ins and outs of the practice.

Free speech for students "is a battle worth fighting," Kalkowski said. "But in no way should students be given absolute free rein. They still need an educated adviser and a strong sense of journalistic integrity."

However, Amster said students should be given a chance to make mistakes, even under the guidance of an adviser.

"There is no way that we can expect students to learn the skills they need to be responsible journalists if we deny them the freedom of speech that 'real' journalists have," Amster said. "We also need to provide them with structure and qualified advisers who will challenge them and make sure that they are learning from their mistakes as well as their successes."

To this end, HighWired.com officials plan to develop suggested publication guidelines for administrators, addressing general policies for online high school newspapers.

| *"Forty-eight percent of administrators disagreed strongly when asked if high school students should be allowed to report controversial issues in the newspaper without approval."*

Many School Administrators Are Ignorant About First Amendment Issues

Laurie Lattimore

In the following viewpoint Laurie Lattimore, who now teaches journalism at Dominican University in California, argues that educating students and teachers about freedom of the press is not enough, because it is the school administrators who are responsible for censorship. Few administrators are interested in the issue of students' First Amendment rights, she says, and most are not well informed about current law. Those who are aware of the Supreme Court's Hazelwood *decision do not understand the details of it, and it is often abused. In some cases, however, principals have supported the school newspaper when censorship was imposed by the school board.*

While informing newspaper advisers and student journalists of their First Amendment rights, don't overlook the administrators.

Given the increasing knowledge of scholastic press rights among students and advisers, it is almost hard to believe high school administrators can have such differing views on the purpose of the student newspaper and their own level of involvement with the production of the newspaper.

Almost.

Unfortunately, the primary audience for First Amendment education in the scholastic press is students and advisers.

"We can preach all we want at the Journalism Educator's Association [JEA] or the Association for Education in Journalism and Mass Communication, but we are just preaching to the choir," said Mike Hiestand of the Student Press Law Center (SPLC), a non-profit organization dedicated to educating students about their First Amendment rights.

Administrators Need to Be Better Educated

It may be the high school administrators who need to hear the sermon the most. While it is crucial to continue informing newspaper advisers and student journalists of their First Amendment rights in light of Supreme Court decisions and legislative actions, it is a grave mistake to overlook those who are often behind the censorship.

But administrators' lack of knowledge is not all for lack of trying. Journalism educators who have attempted seminars and workshops with administrators about student rights and responsibilities have found unenthusiastic audiences, if any audience at all. Candace Perkins-Bowen, scholastic media program coordinator at Kent State University, had planned a workshop for principals during her High School Newspaper Institute this summer [2001]. Of the 35 principals invited for the expense-paid seminar, only six showed any interest.

"We decided that wasn't 'critical mass' enough to devote the expense, so we are just sending them information," Perkins-Bowen said. She noted that JEA also has attempted to host work-

Students at Cypress Bay High School in Weston, Florida, prepare their newspaper for distribution. School administrators across the United States are split over whether students should enjoy greater or lesser degrees of free expression in school newspapers. © AP Images/ Alan Diaz.

shops for administrators, but they have been sparsely attended as well.

Jay P. Goldman, a former education reporter who now edits *The School Administrator*, a monthly magazine, said school law issues—particularly student rights—are issues that administrators are not concerned enough about.

"I don't think anyone would quibble with the fact that administrators need more training," Goldman said. "But it is easy to see why administrators would not flock to these sessions. They have so many demands and there is such intense pressure on performance that they get caught up in test mania and allow other things to slide by."

Goldman said part of the problem is the perception that mainstream media are unfair in education news coverage, which makes administrators fearful of a free student press. "I don't agree with it, but I understand it," he said.

Support from Some Administrators

Alan Weintraub, dean at Westport High School in Massachusetts, is doing his part to convince fellow administrators not to be afraid of the student newspaper but rather to embrace its potential as a magnifying glass into students' lives—a must for high school educators.

"After reading an interview with a teenage alcoholic, a girl who has recently had an abortion, a boy who has tried to commit suicide, or a student who works 40 hours a week and doesn't get home before 11 P.M.," he said, "it is difficult for any of us to ignore that students have complicated lives that have a direct effect on their ability to function in the classroom." . . .

At Hall High School in Connecticut, it was actually the principal who went to bat for the student newspaper when the staff wanted to do a story on a science teacher being investigated for improprieties while giving a standardized aptitude test. The school board attorney said the newspaper could do nothing. If Elaine Bessette—a high school newspaper adviser before going into administration—had not pushed the issue, the staff would have been out of luck.

Student editor Miro Kazakoff, now a computer science and English double major at Georgetown University, believed the student publication, *Hall Highlights*, was obligated to report on the situation. "The principal actually came to our defense when the [school board's] lawyer told us we could not print anything," Kazakoff said. "I was sweating terribly. Half of me was wondering how we would get back the current article since the paper was at the printer; half of me was wondering what we would print there instead."

Though Bessette was unable to convince the attorneys that the student newspaper deserved professional press status when it came to covering the investigation, the paper was allowed to do a story on the gag order. Bessette even gained school board approval for the high school students to do a report once the local newspaper broke the story.

"Personally, I don't think the principal should have any prior review," she said. "If a story is controversial but not illegal, the principal could walk the staff through the possible outcomes so they can decide how to handle it. If the article is critical, it is critical. Tough."

Bessette, currently principal at Greenwhich High School, admittedly falls on the liberal side of the spectrum when it comes to administrative views of student rights. At the other end of the spectrum is Pete McMurray, principal of Itawamba [Mississippi] High School. He confiscated the school's newspapers when he saw a political cartoon depicting an inept school board.

"I wouldn't want anything derogatory in our paper," said McMurray, who spent two years in the U.S. Marines before beginning a 24-year career in secondary education. "The school newspaper is not an arena for free expression. For those students who are serious about journalism, they can do that at the next level."

Legal Confusion

Part of the difficulty for administrators is the inherent subjectivity of the standards put forth in the Supreme Court's landmark *Hazelwood vs. Kuhlmeier* decision. The 1998 decision affects most current high school newsroom environments and grants administrators editorial control of student publications as long as [administrators'] actions are "reasonably related to legitimate pedagogical concerns." What is considered reasonable and/or legitimate is left to one's own interpretation, however, and is likely to be vastly different between students and administrators.

"The Supreme Court has said since principals are government agents, they have to give a reason for censorship," said Mark Goodman, executive director of the SPLC. "*Hazelwood* lowered that standard and said if censorship is merely reasonable, then it is constitutional. The problem is that it is completely subjective what constitutes 'reasonable.'"

Gene Reynolds, who was principal of Hazelwood East High School in 1988 and whose actions led to the lawsuit, claims the Supreme Court decision was not meant to be a mandate for administrative censorship.

VIEWS OF THE AMERICAN PUBLIC TOWARD PRESS FREEDOM

Overall, do you think that Americans have too much press freedom, too little press freedom, or is the amount about right?

	1999	2000	2001	2002
Too much freedom	31%	40%	36%	33%
Too little freedom	17%	14%	13%	13%
About right	49%	43%	47%	51%
Don't know/refused	4%	3%	4%	2%

Taken from: Ken Paulson, "Too Free?" *American Journalism Review*, Sept. 2002. www.ajr.org.

"The *Hazelwood* case did not give us more rights to censor student newspapers, but it did give us more authority," Reynolds told the American Society of Newspaper Editors in March [2001].

Scott Mutchie, superintendent in Clarkston, [Washington], is opposed to the *Hazelwood* standard and remains partial to the First Amendment.

"I don't agree with the Supreme Court on that one," Mutchie said. "As an administrator, I had to watch carefully that administrators did not react to the way students felt. As soon as you say, you can't print that because you don't like it, you are obstructing their freedom of speech."

Chris Richardson, former superintendent of the North Platte School District in Nebraska, supports the *Hazelwood* standard but is quick to admit it is a difficult one for administrators to figure out and easy to abuse.

"Absolutely it is abused," Richardson said. "With the broad way *Hazelwood* is written, an administrator could have lots of objections with something that is negative toward the administration or the school and decide to take it out or place a gag order on the paper."

That is why Richardson is among a growing constituency of high school journalism advocates who are recognizing a need to pull administrators into the journalism education mix: talking to student journalists about responsibilities that come with rights, teaching advisers the standards of solid reporting and good ethics, and of course working with administrators on "reasonable" involvement in the student press.

"I've just got to believe the more educated people are about the current case law and the First Amendment, that will go the longest way in giving our students rights," Richardson said. "Good people with the right education will make good decisions." . . .

The Freedom Forum recently conducted a survey of teachers and administrators on their views of student rights and responsibilities of the First Amendment. When administrators were asked to name which freedoms were guaranteed in the First

Amendment, 77 percent named free speech but only 19 percent named free press and 21 percent said freedom of religion. Four percent thought the right to bear arms was part of the First Amendment. Forty-eight percent of administrators disagreed strongly when asked if high school students should be allowed to report controversial issues in the newspaper without approval from school authorities.

"Teacher and administrator education on the First Amendment is sorely lacking," [Charles Haynes, of the First Amendment Schools project,] said. "Most administrators go into public schools with little or no background on law. But our thinking is that if we give students the opportunity to be responsible, we'll have a better result."

> *"We'd rather have the ideas in print in the school newspaper, where the students can learn to harness their energy, anger, and intensity."*

Giving Students Freedom to Control Their Newspaper Can Improve a High School

Harry Proudfoot and Alan Weintraub

In the following article Harry Proudfoot, the journalism adviser at Westport High School in Massachusetts, and Alan Weintraub, the dean of the school, tell why the decision not to censor the school newspaper has benefited their school. They do not view the paper as a public relations tool, as do many administrators of other schools. The students at Westport have complete control of the newspaper and are therefore more concerned with their responsibilities as journalists than with rights. This condition has had a strong positive impact on the sense of community within the school. Furthermore, the paper's reports on teen problems have made teachers and administrators take steps toward improving students' lives. It has won awards and is considered one of the best high school papers in the nation, even though the school is a small one with a low budget.

W e thought that we knew how big the alcohol problem was among students at Westport High School. We thought it was not as bad as national surveys made student alcohol use out to be. And we had implemented a breathalyzer policy to guarantee that all school social events, at least, were alcohol free. But then the *Villager*, our high school newspaper, did a survey on drinking. It showed us just how wrong we were.

It wasn't that the overall numbers were that bad—albeit worse than we expected. They revealed that our students were just about at the national average in terms of alcohol use. But the paper also asked how often people drank. And that's where the shock was. Some of the students surveyed—who took the survey seriously—said they could not get through a day without a drink.

The *Villager* ran the piece as its cover story that week and later ran an interview with a student who clearly had an alcoholism problem. At Westport High School, we can no longer pretend we don't have an alcohol problem. Our high school newspaper has seen to that.

Many administrators might see that last bit as a problem. After all, no one wants to see negative news items about their school in any newspaper, let alone in a student publication. Isn't the school newspaper supposed to be a public relations tool that showcases the good things that happen? Some schools even try to keep their student papers from printing stories about sports team losses.

We Don't Censor

We don't censor the paper. We don't engage in any form of prior review. The students own the newspaper. They are responsible for what it says and what it does. What they decide matters to them and to the students who read it.

As a result, the *Villager* has become something much more useful than a public relations tool that no one either reads or believes. First, it has had a dramatic impact on school climate. There

The Villager *tackles difficult and controversial issues such as underage drinking without censorship by the school.* © Diverse Images/Universal Images Group/Getty Images.

are student cliques at Westport High School, like every other high school. The difference is ours get along with each other. In part, that's because over the course of the year, members of every subgroup become the topic of some news or feature story in the paper. Part of the *Villager*'s mission statement—a statement the students decided they needed and developed on their own—is to build a greater sense of community within the school. The result is the staff constantly tries to find ways to remind students of their classmates' humanity.

Many of the paper's editorials appear to have a similar aim. They constantly urge all of us to become more respectful of one another. And they are as quick to point out our successes as our failures. Further, they reveal the issues that students confront. After reading an interview with a teenage alcoholic, a girl who has recently had an abortion, a boy who has tried to commit suicide, or a student who works 40 hours a week and doesn't get home before 11:00 P.M. most nights, it is difficult for any of us to ignore that students live complicated lives that have a direct effect on their ability to function in the classroom.

With stories such as these, the *Villager* forces school staff members to take steps toward improving students' lives. Equally important, the *Villager* is an avenue for open and clear communications about where students are coming from. More than once, items in the paper have made both teachers and administrators rethink decisions that have been made.

Not that the students' opinions always make sense. Sometimes their ideas are ridiculous. Sometimes a writer's opinions are so

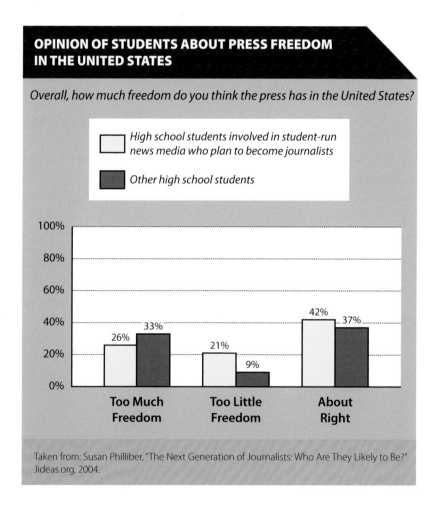

OPINION OF STUDENTS ABOUT PRESS FREEDOM IN THE UNITED STATES

Overall, how much freedom do you think the press has in the United States?

High school students involved in student-run news media who plan to become journalists

Other high school students

Taken from: Susan Philliber, "The Next Generation of Journalists: Who Are They Likely to Be?" Jideas.org, 2004.

negative or idealistic that we wonder what galaxy the writer lives in. But even the most far-out columns serve positive purposes. Sometimes a writer just needs to blow off steam. Sometimes a column is part of the process of growing up—a moment of public adolescent rebellion that eventually leads to greater maturity. Regardless, we'd rather have the ideas in print in the school newspaper, where the students can learn to harness their energy, anger, and intensity, than in an underground publication where that emotional angst just feeds on itself and creates greater negativity in the long run.

High Rank Despite Disadvantages

Of course some will argue that Westport is a special case. We are a small school—barely 500 students. We are a rural school—our town still has more cows than people. We are in Massachusetts—a liberal bastion that cares more for rights than responsibilities. We have a teacher adviser with more than 20 years' experience.

All these things are true. But our adviser has never functioned under prior review anywhere, even when he first started teaching. In fact, in his first year of advising, the newspaper ran a story critical of administrators for terminating three teachers. That paper went on to win national recognition in only his third year of advising in large part because the students' ownership of the paper made them want to excel.

In addition, the staff of the *Villager* is more concerned with responsible action than with rights. Students spend as much time exploring the ethics of their stories as they do creating them. Further, as part of school policy, every *Villager* staff member participates in a detailed discussion of the American Society of Newspaper Editors' Canons and Ethics of Journalism before they write their first story. Every student understands that with his or her right to freedom of the press comes the responsibility to use those rights ethically. And although we are a rural town, we are nestled between two of the most economically depressed cities in America. We have a significant immigrant population, and our students' first language is as often Portuguese as it is English. In addition, there is a deep cultural divide between the working class people in the north end of town and the more wealthy in the south. Finally, although we are a small school, we have one of the poorest school budgets in the state. Teachers are paid $6 [thousand]–$7 thousand less each year than even those in the immediate area.

But despite these considerable disadvantages, the *Villager* is consistently ranked among the best high school newspapers in the United States. The students will tell you they win awards not because they set out to win them, but because they are doing the job of good journalists anywhere: communicating factual information to people in ways that will help them live better lives. They will tell that you they are successful in that pursuit because they have been given the tools they need to succeed and the freedom they need to pursue their mission. And they will tell you that any school can have this kind of newspaper if [it has] the courage to give students ownership of their newspaper.

> *"All news organizations get . . . harassment in trying to cover sensitive stories. But [members of] the student press take a lot more abuse."*

Student Journalists Face Difficulties in Doing Undercover Stories

Don Corrigan

In the following article Don Corrigan, a professor of journalism at Webster University in St. Louis, reports on what high school students experienced while researching a story on tobacco use. They had gone undercover to see what stores in the area would sell cigarettes to minors, and they were advised that to be fair they should get comments from the managers of stores that did. When the manager of one store seized their camera and destroyed their film, the story was reported by a local television channel. Reporters often encounter harassment when covering sensitive stories, but it is more frequent in the case of students. Not all school districts are as supportive as the administration of this one was; many feel that school publications should not print anything negative about local businesses.

When Webster Groves High School student reporters began their undercover story on teen smoking, they never dreamed it would get a "promo" on KSDK (Channel 5). But St. Louis TV news got the scoop on their reporting project after an incident at the local supermarket.

Reporters on the *Echo* student newspaper received television news coverage after their investigation hit a snag at the Schnucks supermarket at 8650 Big Bend Blvd. A manager at the grocery took issue with their reporting, asked for their camera and destroyed film for the story.

"Seizing reporters' film and destroying it is definitely wrong and is certainly a First Amendment issue, which is why TV news probably picked it up," said Donald Johnson, a faculty member at the high school and adviser to the *Echo* newspaper.

Reporter Mike Owens of Channel 5 covered the incident on Monday, Jan. 10 [2000], the lead story on the 10 P.M. newscast. The following Tuesday morning [January 11, 2000], the phones in student newspaper adviser Johnson's office were ringing with more press inquiries.

Also on that Tuesday, Jan. 11 [2000], Schnucks' spokesperson Marie Casey said supermarket officials regretted the incident. Casey said the store co-manager, Jane Cooper, would meet with students for an apology and a gift of five rolls of film. Casey added that free developing would be provided.

"Schnucks regrets this unfortunate incident," said Casey. "Our store's co-manager has acknowledged that she did not handle the situation well."

Harassment of the Press

Mark Goodman, an attorney and the executive director of the Student Press Law Center (SPLC), located in Arlington, [Virginia], lamented that incidents involving harassment of the student press are all too common. SPLC documents such abuses in its quarterly reports. Its staff advises students on their legal rights as journalists.

Taking Photos in Privately Owned Public Places: The Law

As a general rule, reporters have a right to enter privately owned public places (private school campuses, restaurants, shopping malls) without permission but must leave or stop gathering information if asked to do so. Note, however, any photos or other information a reporter obtains prior to being asked to leave belong to the reporter and neither the police nor the property owner has the right to confiscate a camera, film or notebook on the spot.

Law of the Student Press, 2nd edition, Student Press Law Center, 1994.

This is not a problem confined to the student press," said Goodman. "All news organizations get this kind of harassment in trying to cover sensitive stories. But [members of] the student press take a lot more abuse. There's a feeling out there: 'Well, these are just kids pretending to be reporters. This is play journalism.'"

Goodman can cite plenty of "play journalism" by students, that later became big news in the mainstream press. He can also point to legal costs incurred by organizations and companies that failed to recognize that student journalists have First Amendment rights.

Echo reporting students were involved in an undercover reporting project in which under-age students attempted to purchase cigarettes at area stores. Twelve stores were entered, and six sold cigarettes to the minors, according to adviser Johnson. One of those stores selling to minors was the local Schnucks, according to *Echo* editor Amy Cook and project reporters, Hilary Johnson and Katie Zach.

"I was a little surprised when the girls came into the *Echo* office with six packs of cigarettes and asked if they could get reimbursed," said adviser Johnson. "I didn't want them doing anything illegal, and in retrospect, I wish I had told them not to actually purchase cigarettes if the offer was there.

"They came up with the idea of checking out the stores, but it's only a small part of their centerspread on the tobacco problem," said Johnson. "There are also stories on the new city ordinance on tobacco sales, an article with 10 ways to kick the habit and a survey on how many kids are smoking at the high school."

Johnson said the six stores selling tobacco to minors will be named in the story. Johnson said he told the students it was only fair to go back to those six stores and get comments from managers about their policies and what happened with the sales to under-age purchasers.

When the students approached store co-manager Jane Cooper at Schnucks for comment, the incident, involving the camera and destruction of film ensued.

"According to the students, Mrs. Cooper told them that fake IDs must have been used to purchase the cigarettes," noted Johnson. "When the reporters tried to leave the store, she reportedly told them, 'We're going to settle this right here.' That's when she demanded the camera, got the film out and cut it up."

Goodman said the SPLC always advises students not to engage in illegal activities as part of a story. He said undercover stories—such as those involving purchase of tobacco or alcohol by minors—can always present problems.

"We advise that in such stories the students stop right at the point of purchase," said Goodman. "Another option is to tell law enforcement what you are doing, so they are aware of your project. There can be problems with this, however, because reporters don't want to get into the position of doing undercover work for police.

"I think the Webster students can be praised on a number of counts," added Goodman. "They were right to surrender the film rather than to engage in a big confrontation. And they were doing the right thing to return to the grocery to try to get its side

Students at Webster Groves High School were harassed while attempting to complete their undercover investigation of stores that sell tobacco products to minors. © Tim Boyle/Getty Images.

of the story before naming it as a business that sold cigarettes illegally to minors."

Casey, spokesperson for Schnucks, said the store regretted the camera incident and was also investigating the allegation that cigarettes were sold illegally to minors.

"As far as any illegal purchases of cigarettes go, we are issuing a statement to all stores asking clerks to seek identification for anyone who looks age 27 or younger on cigarette sales," said Casey. "Identification must be provided showing that purchasers are 21 years of age.

"Schnucks is investigating the situation of the alleged cigarette sales to the Webster Groves High School minors," added Casey. "If it's discovered that a clerk did not use proper procedure in selling tobacco products, there will be a reprimand."

As SJR [*St. Louis Journalism Review*] went to press, the *Echo* reporting on teen tobacco was slated to appear in the paper's Jan. 31 [2000] issue.

Supportive School Administration

"The problem of illegal sales to minors is a part of what this story project is all about," said Johnson. "The administration here at the high school has been supportive of the project. I told principal Pat Voss right away what was going on when I heard about the sales to minors and the Schnucks incident.

"I frankly expected that there might be some concern about all this hitting when the district has a tax issue coming up," added Johnson. "But I haven't had any pressure from any administrators about this project. Pat Voss said that we have to go about business as usual—we can't second guess ourselves all the time because there is a tax hike coming up on the ballot."

SPLC's Goodman said that school districts are not always so supportive of their school newspapers and the student reporters. Districts do not like student publications giving local businesses a black eye. And some administrators expect high school newspaper advisers to rein in such projects before they get into print.

Goodman cited a similar high school reporting project on tobacco and minors in Blue Springs, [Missouri], that resulted in attempts to censor the school newspaper. The adviser to the school paper was subsequently removed and the students responded with litigation against the district.

"School districts need to have some backbone and support students when they are doing good hard-hitting journalism," said SPLC's Goodman. "Unfortunately, in the aftermath of the 1988 *Hazelwood* ruling by the Supreme Court, many school districts give into the temptation to quash anything that could be controversial."

> "The First Amendment outlaws not merely the most overt and noxious of censorship, the prior restraint, but also after-the-fact retaliation."

Schools Are Turning to Indirect Methods of Discouraging Press Freedom

Frank D. LoMonte

In the following article Frank D. LoMonte, an attorney and the current executive director of the Student Press Law Center, points out that schools now realize that the First Amendment prevents them from direct censorship of student publications unless they can show that the censored content meets the criteria specified by the Supreme Court's Hazelwood *ruling. Therefore, he says, they are turning to other means of restriction. For example, some try cutting back the budget of the student newspaper, firing the faculty adviser, or publicly denouncing articles that have appeared. The First Amendment outlaws retaliation that could discourage future expression of opinions, however, as some but not all courts are deciding; and some states are passing laws that specifically protect teachers and student journalists against it.*

While public school administrators now largely understand that the First Amendment prohibits them from forcing student journalists to withhold or revise disfavored editorial content, that understanding has merely made censorship less overt—not, regrettably, less frequent.

Censorship 2.0 involves pressure indirectly applied: changes to the governance structure of the student newspaper, reassignment (or outright firing) of the faculty adviser, or crippling cuts to the publication budget. These tactics may be subtler than leaning over the student editor's shoulder and pressing the delete key, but they are no less effective.

Fortunately, the law is catching up with the creativity of its would-be evaders. Courts are—with some notable exceptions—recognizing that retaliation by schools and colleges in response to protected speech violates the First Amendment even if the retaliation is indirect.

Courts Grapple with Scope of Student Rights

The Supreme Court's 1988 ruling in *Hazelwood School District v. Kuhlmeier* reaffirmed that, even at the high school level, what students say in school newspapers is protected by the First Amendment. The only question is what showing school administrators must make to justify overriding students' interest in free speech. (Most courts and commentators believe *Kuhlmeier* has no application at the college level, where the state always must establish a compelling interest to legitimize censorship.)

Kuhlmeier coined a two-tiered analysis, applying rigorous scrutiny where student newspapers operate as public forums but relaxed scrutiny where the forum is—through policy or practice—nonpublic.

The First Amendment outlaws not merely the most overt and noxious of censorship, the prior restraint, but also after-the-fact retaliation that is sufficiently severe as to chill a speaker's willingness to engage in future lawful speech. The form that retaliation

A high court ruled that a Connecticut high school could lawfully punish Avery Doninger (center) for making offensive comments online about school administrators, even though the comments were published off campus and in a personal journal. © AP Images/Bob Child.

can take appears to be limited only by the imagination of school administrators.

In a July 2007 ruling, *Husain v. Springer*, the Second Circuit found that officials of New York's College of Staten Island violated the First Amendment rights of student editors by nullifying a student government election in response to what administrators contended was the unfair use of the paper to endorse one party's slate of candidates.

In a ruling issued the same month, *Lane v. Simon* (2007), the Tenth Circuit declined to decide whether students' free speech rights were violated when Kansas State University officials removed their veteran newspaper adviser, claiming dissatisfaction with the "quality" of the publication. Instead of reaching the constitutional issue, the Tenth Circuit merely vacated the district court's finding that no First Amendment violation occurred, ruling that the students' claims became moot when, during the appeal process, they graduated.

Students Find Refuge in State Law

In part because of the uncertain reception their claims will receive in federal court, advocates for student speech rights increasingly are looking to states for relief.

Last year, Oregon became the seventh state to enact a "student free press" statute, declaring that high school and college editors are the ultimate gatekeepers of content in student publications. This assures that students' editorial decisions receive the fullest First Amendment protection recognized in *Kuhlmeier*. A similar initiative, however, stalled in the Washington legislature for the second straight year in the face of opposition from school administrators.

California, the earliest to adopt such a statute, remains the leader in safeguarding the rights of student journalists and is on the verge of enacting the nation's strongest antiretaliation statute explicitly protecting the rights of journalism teachers who speak in defense of what their students publish.

Since 1978, California statutes have outlawed censorship by public schools unless students' speech is "obscene, libelous or slanderous . . . [or] so incites students as to create a clear and present danger" of unlawful or substantially disruptive acts.

Applying that protective statute, California's First Appellate District found in May 2007 that a student author's rights were violated when the school principal and superintendent publicly denounced the student's anti-immigration opinion column, declaring that the column was unprotected speech and never should have been published. By sending the message that "future speech similar to [the column] would not be tolerated," the court held, the officials intimidated the author—and future authors—into refraining from expressing similar viewpoints. *Smith v. Novato Unified School District* (2007).

California's Journalism Teacher Protection Act

In September 2008, California passed the law protecting journalism teachers mentioned in this viewpoint, and it went into effect in January 2009. The following is a portion of the press release issued by the Student Press Law Center at the time the governor signed it.

The Student Press Law Center today congratulated California [Governor] Arnold Schwarzenegger for signing one of the nation's toughest and most forward-looking laws protecting teachers against unfair retaliation when they stand up for their students' First Amendment rights.

"While this law makes the workplace safer for teachers, the real beneficiaries are California's students, who no longer must fear that honest reporting on school events will get their favorite teacher fired," SPLC Executive Director Frank D. LoMonte said. "Governor Schwarzenegger and the California legislature should be commended for sending a message to school officials—in California and across the nation—that teachers are not to be used as pawns to intimidate kids into avoiding legitimate topics of discussion." . . .

California's new law provides that no public school or college employee may be dismissed, suspended, disciplined, reassigned, transferred, or otherwise retaliated against solely for acting to protect a student who is engaged in legally protected conduct. This includes the publication of speech that is not obscene, libelous, slanderous, or substantially disruptive to the safe operations of the school.

Press Release, Student Press Law Center,
September 29, 2008. www.splc.org.

Online Cases Present Ominous Trend

Despite gains made in some state courts and legislatures, this is an anxious time for student journalism. In addition to economic pressures that are causing many high schools to scale back journalism offerings and prompting some collegiate publications to abandon print editions, judicial retrenchment in the protection afforded to online speech casts a long shadow over the ability of students to speak freely even outside of the school day.

In a handful of recent cases, high school administrators have convinced courts that school disciplinary authority should extend to off-campus speech about the school that could reasonably be anticipated to have a disruptive impact if viewed or discussed in school.

In the most worrisome of these cases, *Doninger v. Niehoff* (2008), the Second Circuit ruled in May 2008 that a Connecticut high school could lawfully discipline a student for using a personal online journal to urge the public to contact school administrators—whom she called by an insulting vulgarity—to urge administrators to reverse a decision that threatened a student-organized concert.

The court emphasized that, in its view, Doninger's characterization of the administrators' decisions was misleading and her use of a vulgarity threatened to escalate the dispute, although it is black-letter law that speech does not lose its First Amendment protection either because it is false (unless defamatory, which Doninger's was not) or because it is offensive (a point the Supreme Court reaffirmed in last year's *Morse v. Frederick* ruling [2007]).

While Doninger was not engaged in traditional journalism, the court's ruling is in no way limited to personal blogs. Rather, decisions like *Doninger* portend dangerous times for underground newspapers and other off-campus publications that traditionally have been safe harbors for expression.

Thirty-four years ago, author Jack Nelson wrote in *Captive Voices*, his seminal study of scholastic journalism, that "[c]ensorship is the fundamental cause of the triviality, innocuousness and uniformity that characterize the high school press." Nelson's study fueled the proliferation of independent student periodicals that presaged this generation's online publishing explosion.

Advocates for student journalism must be vigilant that the creep of school authority into students' personal writings does not herald a new era of triviality.

> *"Although public schools can establish*
> *reasonable restrictions as to the time,*
> *place and manner of distribution of*
> *underground publications, they cannot*
> *absolutely forbid their distribution on*
> *school grounds."*

Student Journalists Should Be Aware of Their Legal Rights and Restrictions

Student Press Law Center

The Student Press Law Center, a nonprofit legal aid service for stu-
dent journalists, provides information about freedom of the press
at its website. In the following article it answers the ten questions
high school student journalists most frequently ask about their
rights. It also explains how the Supreme Court's Hazelwood *deci-*
sion applies to student journalists and what kinds of material they
are allowed to publish.

D*o high school students have First Amendment rights?*

Yes. As the United States Supreme Court said in 1969, "It can
hardly be argued that either students or teachers shed their constitutional right to freedom of speech at the schoolhouse gate." But

the First Amendment prohibits only government officials from suppressing speech; it does not prevent school censorship at private schools. A state constitution, statute or school policy could provide private school students with free speech protections.

What about the Hazelwood *decision?*

Hazelwood School District v. Kuhlmeier, the 1988 U.S. Supreme Court decision, gave public high school officials greater authority to censor some school-sponsored student publications if they choose to do so. But the ruling doesn't apply to publications that have been opened as "public forums for student expression." It also requires school officials to demonstrate some reasonable educational justification before they can censor anything. In addition, some states (Arkansas, California, Colorado, Iowa, Kansas, Oregon and Massachusetts) have passed laws that give students stronger free expression protection than *Hazelwood*. Other states are considering such laws.

What is a "public forum for student expression"?

A student publication is a public forum for student expression when school officials have given student editors the authority to make their own content decisions. A school can do that either though an official policy or by simply allowing a publication to operate with editorial independence.

So if policy or practice indicates the content of my publication is determined by students, the Hazelwood *decision doesn't apply to me?*

That's right. If a student publication is a public forum for student expression, then students are entitled to stronger First Amendment protection. School officials are allowed to censor forum publications only when they can show the publication will cause a "material and substantial disruption" of school activities.

STATE LEGISLATION ON STUDENT PRESS RIGHTS

■ State has a free expression law protecting student journalists

■ State has protection for student rights speech in education code

□ A student free expression law has been proposed in the state

■ State lacks added protection for student journalists

Taken from: Student Press Law Center. www.splc.org/knowyourrights/Legislation
_tracking_map.swf.

What about underground or independent student publications? Are they protected from censorship?

Absolutely. Although public schools can establish reasonable restrictions as to the time, place and manner of distribution of underground publications, they cannot absolutely forbid their distribution on school grounds. Like school-sponsored publications that are forums, a school must show substantial disruption before they can censor an independent publication.

Am I in danger of getting sued for defamation or invasion of privacy?

Very rarely, but it can happen, and it's important to observe professional standards if you want your work to be taken seriously. You can't be liable for defamation if you just publish a critical opinion about someone or reveal an unpleasant truth. But if you make a false accusation of fact (even one implied in an "opinion" column), then you may have committed defamation. Invasion of privacy occurs when a publication publicizes embarrassing personal information without consent and with no newsworthy justification, such as gossip about a teacher's marital problems. It can also happen if you mislabel a photo so that it gives a false impression that harms a person's reputation ("false light").

Can we publish students' names and photos online?

Despite what many schools seem to think, no federal privacy law requires a student publication to withhold student information from the Internet or get advance written parental consent (though two states, New Jersey and Maine, appear to do so). If you're told there is such a ban, ask to see the school district policy in writing—and if the policy applies only to sites hosted on a school server (many do), see if you can get your news site hosted on a third-party server like my.hsj.org.

Can I use Freedom of Information laws?

Yes. Freedom of Information, or "sunshine" laws, require government agencies such as public schools to open many of their

A co-editor works on an underground school newspaper in Everett, Washington. Although school administrators may limit how students distribute independent newspapers on campus, they cannot ban them outright. © AP Images/The Herald, Jason Fritz.

official records and meetings to the public. These laws vary from state to state. Every newsroom should have a copy of the state's open records and open meetings laws—a great state-by-state guide is available on the Reporters Committee for Freedom of the Press website.

Can I use cartoon characters, song lyrics or a theme from a popular magazine in my publication?

In most cases, only when you have obtained the permission of the copyright holder. Each of these works is protected by copyright law, which means others can use them only if they have obtained permission. Publishing a credit line does not take the place of permission. There is an exception to copyright law called "fair use" that can apply if you are only using a small amount of a copyrighted work in a way that does not substitute for viewing (or buying) the original.

Am I allowed to reuse photos from Facebook, or MySpace, or videos from YouTube?

It all depends on what you're using them for. It's safest if you are critiquing the material—such as a "funniest videos" highlight segment on a broadcast, where you're adding your own commentary, or if you're making a parody or a mash-up that just "samples" other people's material as an ingredient in a brand-new creative work. The danger goes up with the commercial value of what you're using, so an AP photo published in a celebrity magazine is much riskier than an amateur Facebook photo.

> *"If you are a reporter or photographer, the law says that you are personally responsible for all of your actions while gathering the news."*

Student Journalists Must Report Responsibly to Avoid Lawsuits

Mike Hiestand

In the following article Mike Hiestand, an attorney who specializes in legal issues that affect the high school and college student press, explains that student journalists are legally responsible for what they publish and can be sued if it is libelous. Editors, he warns, must be even more careful, as they are accountable not only for what they write but for what they edit or approve. Suits against students are rare, Hiestand says, because most students do not have enough money to be worth suing. Nevertheless, it is important to be aware of the responsibility that comes with freedom.

After discussing the essential role of a free and independent press and explaining the important legal protections guaranteed by the First Amendment, here is a good Day One homework assignment for your publication staff:

"Write the following 50 times: 'I am legally responsible for *everything* that I write or help to publish.'"

It is a sometimes sobering—but absolutely necessary—wake up call to which many high school student journalists are dangerously oblivious.

The message is this: If you are a reporter or photographer, the law says that you are personally responsible for all of your actions while gathering the news and any material that you subsequently publish. For example, if you have written a news story or column or penned an editorial cartoon that contains serious and sloppy factual errors or if you have taken a photograph of someone in a private place you can be held liable for your mistakes.

If you are an editor, the responsibility is even greater. You can be held legally accountable for all content in which you played a part in publishing. For instance, you are responsible not just for the stories that you personally wrote, but also for all copy that you edited. If you carelessly missed catching a serious factual error in a news story submitted by one of your reporters or if you approved the placement of a misleading photograph you are liable for those mistakes. Additionally, you can be held responsible for content mistakes that appear in advertisements, letters to the editor, guest columns and any other material that you decide to publish. Big note: you are responsible for such material even though you didn't write or create it yourself. (The law may be different for material that is published solely online.)

Who is and isn't potentially liable will depend on who was in the chain of responsibility for publishing the material. For example, if a story about the football coach published in the sports section turns out to be libelous, the following student staffers are potentially liable: (1) the reporter(s) who wrote the story, (2) the sports page editor who did most of the editing and (3) the editor in chief, who is ultimately responsible for all content in the newspaper. The entertainment page editor, for one, would not be liable if he or she played no part in publishing the story.

Student Journalists Are Rarely Sued

While student editors and reporters are fair targets in a lawsuit involving the content of their student publication, they are typically not very attractive ones. In lawyer's lingo they are usually what is called "judgment-proof." In other words, while someone unlawfully harmed by a story may be able to win a multi-million dollar libel case against a student journalist in court, they are not likely going to be able to collect on their judgment. As the saying goes, you can't get water from a stone, and most students are lucky to have enough money in their pocket for lunch, let alone adequate funds to pay off a major award for legal damages.

Bringing a libel lawsuit can be eye-wateringly expensive. It is not uncommon for experienced libel attorneys to charge in excess of $200 an hour for their time. And pursuing a libel claim—especially if it goes to court—takes a lot of time. For that reason, before deciding to bring a lawsuit, lawyers and their cli-

Student journalists are legally responsible for everything they write, although students rarely have enough money to make lawsuits against them worthwhile. © AP Images/The Detroit News, Brandy Baker.

ents usually investigate the financial background of the person or entity they are looking to sue to see if they have sufficient assets available to make a lawsuit feasible. Because penniless students rarely—on their own—justify the time and expense required to file a lawsuit, a person suing will usually try to claim that there were others in the chain of responsibility who should also be held liable for the students' unlawful content. In their quest for a "deep pocket," lawyers will usually also target publication advisers, other school employees, the school system and sometimes even parents.

Fortunately, lawsuits against high school student media are extremely rare. In fact, to date, there are no published court decisions in which a high school has ever been held liable for material published by its student media. Consequently, there is scant law on the topic. There are, however, a number of cases involving public college student media that could provide helpful guidance. These cases have made clear that as long as college employees—including advisers—maintain a hands-off policy with regard to final content decisions, they will not be included in the chain of responsibility and the assets of the school itself cannot be tapped. Courts in such cases have said that advisers can still provide advice, but they must leave the ultimate decisions regarding content and publication to the student staff.

Successful lawsuits against parents are almost unheard of. Parents cannot be held liable for their child's speech merely because of the parental relationship—they must have done something wrong themselves. For example, if a mother edits her child's underground newspaper, she would be in the chain of responsibility for that publication just like any other editor. While that's fairly straightforward, a recent Pennsylvania case created a new—and more problematic—theory for parental liability. There a court held that the parents of a 14-year-old boy who published an especially vile and defamatory website were liable for the "negligent supervision" of their son because they knew about his website yet failed to take sufficient steps to control their

Students Need to Learn the Ethics of Journalism

Is there any real harm if the content and tone of school newspapers is left to the judgment of students? Ironically, without oversight, the student newspaper experience could end up painting a picture that is totally unlike that on a real newspaper. Whereas a journalist writing for a mainstream newspaper will have an editor's supervision to ensure factual accuracy and ethical commitment, the student journalist—especially on an underground newspaper—will likely have no editor or a student editor with neither the training or the incentive to rein in a peer. Where a mainstream newspaper has an economic incentive (in the form of lawsuit for defamation) to avoid statements that denigrate and humiliate others for sport, students, who have little to offer in the way of money damages, are seldom targets in lawsuits when someone's character is destroyed. Sixteen-year-old high school students (and even twenty-year-olds) do not know everything about the contours of the First Amendment or the ethics in the field of journalism. Without meaningful constraint, those within range of the student publication can become subject to a verbal flaying constrained only by the appetite of the perpetrator. . . .

Student journalists merely reflect what they see in the world. If meanness and lack of basic humanity permeate much of popular culture, this is what students will publish. Of course, this merely perpetuates a downward spiral, as the next journalist believes the next article must be even more outrageous and irreverent. . . .

There is an ethical component to one's duty both as a citizen and as a journalist, and learning about how to manage that would seem to be one of the most important lessons any student could learn. Thus, *Hazelwood* may not necessarily be as harmful for students as its critics claim.

Anne Profitt Depre, Speaking Up: The Unintended Costs of Free Speech in Public Schools. *Cambridge, MA: Harvard University Press, 2009. pp.104–106.*

son's conduct. The case is the first—and only—reported decision holding parents liable for their child's speech, and the judge in this case—perhaps because of the especially troubling speech at issue—probably pushed the law further than it actually goes.

The liability message to students should be sent not to frighten, but to alert. With a little knowledge—and a lot of common sense—legal problems can be avoided. As mentioned above, lawsuits against high school student media are exceedingly rare. So while it's important to be careful, journalists do neither themselves nor their readers a favor by being legal "scaredy cats." It is essential that an appropriate balance be struck. Recognizing that with freedom comes responsibility is probably the biggest single step towards getting the balance right

> *"Even as a kid reporter for my newspaper, I felt more paralyzed than liberated by my freedom."*

Views Toward Press Freedom Have Changed

Personal Narrative

Dave Munger

In the following post from his blog, Dave Munger, a journalist who founded ResearchBlogging.com, recalls learning about freedom of the press from an adviser when he was a reporter for his high school newspaper, where no censorship existed. He notes that although the school paper had since created a website, he recently found to his dismay that it had been taken down. He notes that there have been comments on other blogs about how kids do not understand their constitutional rights, but it seems that now they do not have even the rights that they used to have. Moreover, some students, including Munger when he was a student journalist, want restrictions. Munger ultimately acknowledges, though, that such an impulse is not right.

Whereas I was a cub reporter on my high school newspaper, our adviser did one of the few good things he'd ever done for us: he explained freedom of the press. He did a good job of it, too—I still remember what he told us after all these years. Freedom of the press wasn't just some abstract concept: it reached all the way down to us peons writing for the *Garfield Messenger* and printing it in the old A.B. Dick presses in the graphics room down the hall.

You see, he told us, freedom of the press meant we had real freedom, even us kids. But we also had responsibility. We could print whatever we wanted—anything—and there was nothing the principal or anyone else could do to stop us. That was called "prior restraint," and it wasn't allowed, even for a bunch of geeky highschoolers. We could be disciplined afterwards, and the printed papers could even be removed if what we wrote caused a disruption at school, but no one could censor what we wrote before it went to press.

A few months back I did a search for "Garfield Messenger" online and was surprised to find that they now had a very impressive Web site, well designed, with up-to-date articles. As I was writing this post, I looked for the site again, and found it. Unfortunately, now there is only a two-sentence notice, "At the request of *Messenger* staff adviser Steve Miranda, this site has been taken down. We hope to restore it soon."

Steve Miranda was not the adviser back when I wrote for the paper. I don't know what our adviser would have done if we'd had a Web site back in those days. How can there be "prior restraint" with a Web site? Once it's up, it's up. It could be up for 30 seconds, then taken down because of potential for disruption.

There's been some commentary around the blogosphere about how high school students these days don't understand their constitutional rights or don't believe they are reasonable, how many kids don't approve of freedom of speech.

As one student pointed out to *Boing Boing* [an online magazine], many rights don't apply to kids. No freedom of speech, or assembly, or from search and seizure for them. That's part of why I was so amazed that we *did* have freedom of the press. But now, with the Internet washing away the concept of prior restraint, it seems kids no longer have even that.

John Shirley makes an excellent point [in his blog] about the dual world kids live in.

> Usually parental types (I've got three sons) push for more conservative—that is, careful—behavior. But some of these kids seem to have a hunger to restrict freedoms, free speech. Why? Recently a teen we know told my wife that he wished he "had more restrictions." But he kicks if anyone tries to really restrict him. You hear that a lot—young people at once resenting limits and craving them. Could be they're quietly freaked out by the wilderness feeling that the world gives them—mass media and the financial landscape seem, together, a land of wilderness, more a jungle than ever, a sickening plethora of vapid choices.

I was going to add "these days" to my lead-in, but I think it's always been that way. Even as a kid reporter for my newspaper, I felt more paralyzed than liberated by my freedom. Wouldn't it just be easier if they told what we could and could not print? If they treated us like kids all the time, instead of picking and choosing?

It might have been easier, but it wouldn't have been right. I don't know why the *Messenger* has been taken offline, but I hope these kids get back at least that one freedom soon.

UPDATE: The *Messenger's* Web site was back up as of noon today [February 3, 2005].

> *"When student editors ask that the final power be given to them, I think: 'You are asking for a legal right that I don't have, and have never had.'"*

Students Want Rights Professional Journalists Do Not Have

Bruce Ramsey

In the following viewpoint Bruce Ramsey, a columnist for the Seattle Times, *points out that it is not reasonable for students to be given full control of school newspapers, as that is a right that he and other professional journalists do not have. What reporters, columnists, and editors write is printed only at the discretion of the owner of the newspaper they work for. A school paper is owned by the school district. People call it censorship when a principal blocks publication of an article because a school district is a governmental body, yet the principal of a school is merely acting as a manager, just as any publication has a manager representing its owner. In Ramsey's opinion, giving all the power to the students would not prepare them for what they will meet in the real world.*

A bill in Olympia [the capital of Washington State], HB 1307, would give student editors at public high schools control of school papers and other media. The bill's sponsor, [Democrat Representative Dave Upthegrove] Des Moines, said it would extend freedom of the press to students.

In America, freedom of the press belongs to the person who owns one. Consider this column. I drafted it, but it is printed subject to the discretion of The Seattle Times Company and is an exercise in the company's First Amendment rights. It's similar at all newspapers. So, when student editors ask that the final power be given to them, I think: "You are asking for a legal right that I don't have, and have never had. You can forget it."

This was the subject of a legislative hearing and a forum arranged by the Washington News Council. The forum opened with the key question: Who owns the student press? The bill's

Students walk the halls in a Seattle, Washington, high school. A bill to give students in Washington State greater ownership over their school newspaper would give them a level of control even professional journalists don't have. © AP Images/Ted S. Warren.

supporters said the people owned it, the readers owned it or the students owned it, or some minestrone of the above. Eddie Reed, math specialist at the Tukwila School District, set them straight: "The school district owns it."

Then it should serve the school district's purposes: education, an activity that requires adult supervision.

But there is a problem. The school district is part of government. Brian Schraum, a Washington State University student, said, "I believe the government should never be involved in the editorial process." Several people quoted the newspaper editor's old line: "When I do it, it's editing. When the government does it, it's censorship."

A School Principal Acts as a Manager, Not a Censor

And when the principal of a public high school does it, what is it? By profession, the principal is neither a publisher nor a censor. He's a manager. When he does it, it's management—the same as in a private school.

A good principal will wield his pen lightly, keeping in mind that the main purpose of the school paper is to educate the students who write it.

"I have never censored an article," said Jonathan Kellett, principal of Stadium High School in Tacoma. But he recalled a case in which he would have blocked a letter to the editor, had he been principal. It was an anonymous letter from a girl alleging racial intimidation on a school bus—a case too serious to be handled that way.

Mike Hiestand, consulting attorney for the Student Press Law Center of Arlington, [Virginia], said Kellett was a reasonable principal, but that many principals weren't. But is the solution to that problem to give the legal power to the student?

"We're talking young pups here," said Reed.

HB 1307 would give students the entire power at public colleges and most of the power in public high schools—which is where the controversy is. It would allow the high-school principal to read the paper before going to press and to make changes to avoid libel, invasion of privacy or incitement to disruption. If he changed anything, he and the school district could face a lawsuit for going beyond these exceptions. If he changed nothing, all the liability would be held by the student editor (and perhaps his parents).

The students who spoke for the bill said they were willing to take the responsibility. But when a teenager says, "I'll take the responsibility," what does it mean? Maybe not a lot.

Most interesting was the attitude of the teachers. They all supported the bill. Though it would leave a teacher with no more legal power than the principal, legal power is not the only kind of power there is. The teacher is with the students. Often the conflicts over what can be printed are between the teacher and the principal.

Really, this is a bill to enhance the power of journalism teachers. It allows the students to pretend they are adult journeymen, which they are not, and allows the teachers to get the principals off their backs. It has little to do with the world those students will inhabit if they go to work for a real newspaper.

> *"Censorship simply doesn't work. Today's generation of students is so connected through the cyber world that word travels almost at the speed of thought."*

A Principal Changes His Mind About Censorship

Personal Narrative

Michael Murray

In the following viewpoint Michael Murray, who is superintendent of the Suttons Bay Public Schools in Michigan, tells how his views on freedom of the press for high school students have evolved. He explains that at one time he viewed the student newspaper not as a public forum, but a place to further the school's educational goals. Murray describes how his mind was changed and how he has changed the culture in his school and within the journalism classes to empower his students.

I was not always a champion of freedom of the press for high school newspapers. When the editors of the school newspaper wanted to name the culprits in a high-profile disciplinary case, I argued that my role as principal was to ensure the success of each student. The public shaming would create an atmosphere where the students would not want to return.

Using the standards set by the U.S. Supreme Court in its 1988 ruling in the *Hazelwood* case, I argued the student newspaper was not a public forum, nor did the publishing of student names further the school's educational goals. The editors and I were on opposite sides of the matter. The adviser, not yet tenured, was put in an extremely awkward spot.

Life has a way of throwing events in your path that provide an opportunity to grow or to fossilize.

Confrontational Start

The controversial coverage involved an incident that had taken place at 2 A.M. on a Sunday morning. Students from my high school confronted students from a prominent private school in a parking lot of a junior high to settle a long-simmering feud that had erupted several times on the basketball courts over the previous two years.

The nature of the dispute escalated rapidly when bat-wielding students from the private school emerged from the nearby woods, and one of the public school students ended up in the emergency room with a broken jaw. Several of the private school students were members of a football team contending for a state title.

The local newspaper, the high school paper and the private school's newspaper did not cover the confrontation. The police were stymied by the lack of identities to question. The junior high school students under my charge had eyewitness reports and wanted to cover the story in detail. The superintendent directed us to leave the story alone.

Powerful Point

That is the moment when it became clear to me these young people were going to be learning a powerful lesson about journalism. Is the truth subordinate to political expediency and interest groups? How much are reporters willing to risk to print the truth?

Print it they did, amidst a great deal of emotion and controversy. The local daily then picked up the story and followed it through to the court appearances of two student perpetrators.

If I thought that active backing of the editors of the school paper would make me a hero in the eyes of the students, I was quite mistaken.

At the end of the school year, the 9th graders do a rite of passage known as the Freshman Project. The mother of the editor-in-chief sought me out during the displays to be sure I read her daughter's project on freedom of the student press. The student's message was that I always stressed that people should be judged on what they do, not by what they say. The fact I reviewed the content of each issue before it went to press said a lot about the level of respect and trust I had for the student journalists.

This epiphany led to my next revelation about dealing with student publications. The community expected the principal be in firm control of the school. This meant ensuring nothing controversial or unpopular ever appeared in the school press. In an active community, on almost any issue, there is guaranteed to be a faction that feels the school has no right to express a viewpoint contrary to its espoused beliefs.

Until then, principals in our school district had routinely reviewed student content prior to publication to ensure nothing in print would upset anyone. Consequently, the student paper sat in piles untouched as no students had any interest in reading it. Students viewed the newspaper as little more than student-produced fluff.

Trust Building

The idea of being a censor rankled me on several levels. From a practical standpoint, censorship simply doesn't work. Today's generation of students is so connected through the cyber world that word travels almost at the speed of thought. MySpace,

Facebook, text messaging, instant messaging, cell phone conversations, photos, videos and YouTube videos all have proven too powerful for even the most advanced dictatorships of the world to control.

Students judge adults by what they do, not by what they say. How can an educational leader teach responsible journalism and free press unless the practice reflects the stated philosophical position? There had to be a better way.

As it turns out, there is, but it requires a lot more investment of time and energy. The first step is to establish a relationship with students based on respect and trust. This does not happen overnight but is the cumulative result of decisions and actions.

The next step is to create a culture in the school and, most importantly, in the journalism classes where intellectual curiosity and critical thinking are celebrated. Student culture must be infused with the desire to examine ideas in terms of critical thinking principles: clarity, accuracy, precision, relevance, depth, breadth, logic, significance and fairness.

Finally, a structure must be created in school to support mutual respect and understanding of differing viewpoints. In my case, the journalism class asked for regular press conferences with me so that ideas could be discussed, and the complexity of issues could be explained before stories were completed for the next issue of the newspaper.

On distribution day, I would receive my copy at the same time as the rest of the school with little knowledge of what was covered. From time to time, the student journalists would criticize a school policy or a decision I had made as principal. Still, I felt a sense of pride [because] these criticisms followed a free exchange of ideas that's essential to a democracy, and the articles were written after the students considered opposing viewpoints.

These students are well on their way to becoming the type of citizens we all reference in our vision statements. Being the occasional target of student criticism is a small price to pay for achieving that goal.

> "They [the parent-teacher organization]
> have a list of demands that we have
> respectfully reviewed with open minds.
> But . . . the demands are not reasonable."

Press Freedom Is Being Lost

Personal Narrative

Becky Metrick

In the following viewpoint Becky Metrick, an editor of the student newspaper at Lakeridge High School in Lake Oswego, Oregon, argues that the local parent-teacher organization's objections to an article about drugs in the paper are unjustified. The staff knew the article was controversial, she says, so they were very careful to make sure that it did not promote drug use. Nevertheless, the parents were outraged by it and took the issue to the school board, which is now reconsidering the school's policy of not censoring the paper. Metrick believes that the staff did nothing wrong and that publishing the article was within their rights under the Constitution.

For the first time in my high school journalism career, the free press rights our newspaper staffers and I have as student journalists at Lakeridge High School have come into question.

It all began when we printed an opinion piece by senior Tyler Smith on psychedelic drugs in our Jan. 13 [2009] issue of the *Newspacer*.

Smith wrote about how these drugs are often considered different, and more spiritual, than most other drugs used. Smith was very careful in putting down precise facts, getting many interviews and sticking exactly to explaining what it was that made them different. He in no way implied that drugs were OK or promoted them.

Unfortunately, a parent group in our community, the Waluga Parent-Teacher Organization, believed that the article did.

As a reporter and editor, I know that as a newspaper staff, we were very careful about that article because we understood it could be controversial. We worked to make sure that it did not promote drugs in any way, as that would not be under our First Amendment rights.

It went through many hard edits, and sadly, because of space limitations in the layout, we had to cut the article to about half its original length.

This might have taken out some of the clarity, but even after consulting a lawyer, we see ourselves as within our rights.

The WPTO was outraged with the subject matter, and has officially taken the matter to the school board. They have a list of demands that we have respectfully reviewed with open minds. But in terms of professionalism, the demands are not reasonable.

We have done our best to address this calmly and carefully, because we don't want to make things worse than they are. I know that we were within our rights as a paper, but the WPTO interprets the laws differently than we do.

Free Press Rights

Our paper follows the state policy for student newspapers, which gives us the same free press rights as professional papers. The only subjects we cannot cover are ones that will "incite a clear and present danger" to the students.

The WPTO went to the school board recently about the issue, in hopes that the district will review and change its policy on student publications. At the school board meeting tonight, our staffers will have a chance to speak, defend ourselves and present arguments about why we want to renew the current policy.

In addition to that, Smith, a senior, wrote a clarification in our most recent Feb. 12 [2009] issue that clearly explained his intentions. He also apologized to a freshman with the same Tyler Smith name, who erroneously received criticism for writing the article.

I feel that my paper is not at fault for anything and believe we have strong protection in our free press rights. Although I understand why parents might be concerned, I do not read the article as promoting drugs or telling students to do them. We are a high school paper, and covering topics like this may be controversial, but it is something that is relevant in today's society and to our school.

I will be at the school board meeting, and hopefully, we'll be able to prove to the board that we have done nothing wrong, and convince them to keep the current policy.

The paper writes about things the students want to read about, and we pride ourselves on being as professional as possible. This issue has been extremely frustrating, but we are focusing on being respectful and mature while confronting it. We have received support from many other parents, community members and even other local publications.

We believe in our paper, and the reporters believe in the words they write and publish. I hope this issue doesn't force us to change that.

> "Schools should encourage students to express themselves freely, as a way to teach students to peacefully accept and tolerate different beliefs."

Censorship of Student Journalists Is Harmful and Wrong

Personal Narrative

Carrie Courogen

In the following viewpoint, Carrie Courogen says that she wrote an article on censorship for her school newspaper that was itself censored so that she had to print and distribute it on her own. She declares that students' rights under the Constitution are being restricted more and more because of administrators' belief that they should protect younger students from controversial material. Yet teens are constantly told that school is preparing them for the real world, and in the real world, they will be exposed to plenty of controversy. Individuals of all ages have freedom of choice as to what to read, she argues; they do not have to read anything in the paper that they do not want to, and so students should not be prevented from expressing their opinions. Courogen was a senior at

Camp Hill High School in Pennsylvania in 2009, when this article was published.

Last year, I wrote an article about censorship in schools for my own school newspaper after witnessing countless great ideas shot down because they were considered to be "too controversial."

Ironically, after being told that if I made the requested changes it would be printed, the newspaper adviser censored my article about censorship. When I asked why it was not in the issue, I was told that the subject material did not concern, nor was appropriate for, the student body. Outraged, I printed out my own copies and distributed the article myself.

The U.S. Constitution's Bill of Rights has existed for 220 years. The Bill of Rights grants American citizens the most basic of all civil rights and liberties: freedom of religion, freedom of the press and several others.

But most importantly, the Bill of Rights grants the freedom of speech and expression, a right that should not be taken for granted. These rights are guaranteed to all American citizens, but in the last 50 years, certain restrictions have been placed on them.

School environments have been restraining students through acts of censorship that infringe on students' rights to free speech and expression. It is becoming more and more difficult to wear a shirt [bearing a controversial message or image] or write an article without being punished for it.

These acts of censoring minors should no longer be accepted as correct; rather, they should be viewed as undemocratic and unnecessary.

The topic of censorship of minors arose during the controversial era surrounding the Vietnam War, when the U.S. Supreme Court ruled in favor of a group of student protesters, saying that students should not be required to check their basic rights, such as freedom of speech, at school doors.

The court declared that in school environments, students still retain their rights, as long as they are not causing a disruption and are expressing themselves in a peaceful manner. However, student rights were infringed upon when the Supreme Court ruled in the *Hazelwood v. Kuhlmeier* case that censorship of school newspapers was constitutional.

The main argument for censorship is that all constitutional rights are relative, but not absolute. If school districts deem something inappropriate, they have a responsibility to protect the rights of the majority before the rights of the minority. High schools are comprised of students from the ages of 14 to 18; the younger ones need to be protected from controversial material.

Controversy Exists in the Real World

Although schools need to protect those who might not want to view something a student might have written, censoring the student is not the answer. Almost every day, we as high school students are being reminded that we are being prepared for "the real world."

Well, I hate to be the bearer of bad news, but there's a lot of controversy in the real world, and sooner or later teenagers are going to be subjected to it. The age of reason is seven, and students are given another right: the freedom of choice. No one forces students to read something they don't want to. They have the freedom to choose what they want to view. Certainly high school students have the sensibility to know what they want to view and what they don't.

This is not an argument against censorship for students who want to express controversial ideas simply for the sake of controversy. It's not so students can print obscenities and claim that it's OK because they have the freedom of speech or write gossip columns that infringe on other students' rights to privacy. This argument is about protecting opinions.

We spent our childhood being told to have our own views and ideas. Why is it that when we transcend into high school, suddenly our opinions are repressed just because they might offend someone else? Instead of exercising unreasonable censorship, schools should encourage students to express themselves freely, as a way to teach students to peacefully accept and tolerate different beliefs. By limiting these rights, schools are doing more harm than good.

Students should not be asked to abandon their rights at school doors. They should not be the subjects of constant censorship [by] school officials. The school environment is one of the few places that students should feel comfortable expressing themselves in an effort to grow and mature intellectually.

Schools are hurting their students by censoring them, not helping them. Although schools think they have students' best interests in mind, they are really infringing on their basic rights.

> "A significant and positive relationship
> exists between those who use online
> sources for information and news and
> the perception that the press is not
> given more rights than it deserves."

Students Who Write Online Favor More Freedom of the Press than Those Who Do Not

Kenneth Dautrich, David A. Yalof, and Mark Jose López

In the following excerpt from their book, The Future of the First Amendment, *Kenneth Dautrich and David Yalof, who are associate professors at the University of Connecticut, and Mark Jose López, who is a research associate professor at the University of Maryland, discuss the impact of online activity on student attitudes toward freedom of the press. Students who use digital media to express their own opinions are not as likely as other students to think the press has too much freedom, they say. Those who write blogs or participate in chat rooms and online discussions, or who simply read news on the Internet, tend to be more supportive than others of First Amendment rights in general. In the authors' opin-*

ion, this difference shows that digital media are an effective form of civic education.

The digital media not only open up access to a plethora of news and information sources but also dramatically extend the ability to publish. Many high school students are taking advantage of these publishing opportunities. Are those who are taking advantage of the digital media by publishing becoming more supportive and appreciative of the constitutional principles that protect the rights of expression?

Does the First Amendment Go Too Far?

Those who are frequent users of digital media to express their own opinions are least likely to disagree that the First Amendment goes too far in the rights it guarantees, and [they] are the most likely to have offered an opinion, even once observed factors are controlled. This suggests that those who use digital media technologies to express their opinions are more supportive of, and are more likely to have formed an opinion about, the First Amendment than those who do not use these digital media sources frequently.

On the issue of whether the press has an excess of freedom, the data show that participation in online discussions and the posting of material to blogs has a positive and statistically significant relationship with the feeling that the press does not have too much freedom to do what it wants. Specifically, 49 percent and 48 percent, respectively, of those who do not chat online and do not post material to blogs say the press has either the "right amount" or "too little" freedom in America. By contrast, 54 percent of those who do participate in online conversations and 56 percent of those who post material to blogs offer this opinion about the press's freedom. Those engaging in online publishing are, in fact, more sensitive to restrictions on the behavior of the press, even once observed confounding factors are controlled.

The fact that individuals who publish their ideas through online conversations and blogs are more favorable toward press freedoms suggests that engaging in digital publishing may have the effect of promoting support for press freedoms. . . .

Dimensions of Support for Free Expression

Generally, the greater the use of chat rooms and online discussions, the more students are willing to support free expression rights. And the relationships are similar in magnitude; that is, the percentage improvement in agreement, from those who do not chat to those who are frequent chatters, is in the range of five to eight points, all of which is statistically significant without any confounding factors controlled, and from one to five points when these factors are controlled, in some cases showing a wider gap.

There is also a clear influence of publishing through postings on blogs. The more frequently students engage in posting

A study showed that high school students are less tolerant of free speech than the adult population. Those who maintain a blog, however, are less likely to take their First Amendment rights for granted. © AP Images/Adam Bird.

material on blogs, the more they say they support free expression across all five of the dimensions that we measured. The magnitude of the relationships appears highest on the press-specific items, where the spread between those who do not post and those who frequently post is nine percentage points, even once observed factors are controlled. This suggests a very strong relationship between blogging and support for free expression and media rights.

Again, the experience of using these digital media to publish materials does appear to have a corresponding positive influence on heightened support for free expression rights. The act of publishing makes students more appreciative and supportive of free expression, particularly as it relates to press rights. These findings suggest that as students continue to engage in online publishing, they may come to better appreciate free expression rights.

To What Extent Is the First Amendment Taken for Granted?

Finally, [we] address the question of whether online publishing leads students to be more reflective of their First Amendment rights. Two findings are noteworthy in this regard. First . . . more frequent blog posting and more frequent online chatting are related to having an opinion and thinking about the issue of whether or not one takes his or her rights for granted. For example, 45 percent of those who never participate in online discussions say they do not know how to answer this question, compared to 32 percent of those who frequently participate in chat rooms. Second, at least with respect to posting material on blogs, it does appear that frequency of this behavior leads to the development of an attitude toward more personally thinking about First Amendment rights: 22 percent of nonbloggers say they personally think about their rights, while 28 percent of frequent bloggers say the same.

It is important to note here, however, that controlling confounding factors mitigates the relationship between online chatting and views of the rights guaranteed by the First Amendment. Specifically, once observable factors are controlled, frequency of chat room use is unrelated to students' views of the rights guaranteed by the First Amendment.

Naturally, one would expect the beneficiaries of freedom to stand tall among its greatest defenders. High school students, who must navigate a litany of restrictions and rules every day both at home and at school, should be first and foremost among them. Yet, FOFA [*Future of the First Amendment*] 2004 revealed some sobering truths about high school students in particular: they tend to be less tolerant of First Amendment expression than school teachers, school principals, and even the adult population as a whole in many instances. FOFA 2004 revealed that students who participate in student media tend to be more supportive of these freedoms. Unfortunately, so few students participate (no more than 10 percent participate in any school-authorized media activity) that a less tolerant and more apathetic ethos prevailed in the nation's high schools: Nearly three fourths of students in 2004 either said they didn't know how they felt about the First Amendment or that they took it for granted.

Impact of the Digital Media Revolution on High School Students

The digital media revolution of recent years has influenced the way many institutions in democracy work. Members of Congress trade e-mails with constituents and accept campaign contributions via the Internet; Supreme Court opinions can be distributed across the globe within seconds and invite criticisms and controversy within minutes; the president of the United States is the subject of thousands of online diaries chronicling his every move. What about high school students, who in many cases are even more technologically savvy than the adults? What type of impact has the digital media revolution had on them, and more specifically, how, if at all, has it affected their appreciation and support for free expression rights? FOFA 2006 offered numerous ways of measuring the degree to which new media users, be they those who consume online media or who participate in and create new media, tend to support the very First Amendment freedoms that buttress their activities.

As it turns out, the more intense digital media users are more aware of the role they play in the so-called "marketplace of ideas," and they are more likely to defend the freedom of that marketplace than those who interact with digital media less often. In assessing those who use the digital media as a source of news and information, data from FOFA 2006 revealed that a significant and positive relationship exists between those who use online sources for information and news and the perception that the press is not given more rights than it deserves. Beyond just support for free press rights, those who more regularly use the Internet to get information tend to be highly associated with support for all sorts of free expression rights. Certainly, not all Internet sites are the same. In contrast, we found that those who rely on blogs for news do not exhibit the same level of support for free expression rights as those who gather information regularly from more "established" Internet websites. Perhaps that's because they're searching for opinions rather than searching for "news" per se. Still, the overall connection between Internet usage and support for free expression rights appears to be a strong one.

What about the millions of bloggers who create online diaries? Their numbers are not small: thanks to MySpace.com and other social-networking sites that are growing substantially, it has never been easier for the nation's high school students to e-mail, chat online, and post their opinions in a place where the public can consume them. Certainly, FOFA 2006 reveals that bloggers, as well as those who participate in online discussions, tend to think the press in America does not have enough freedom to publish. In fact, online publishers, who now number in the tens of millions, are more sensitive to restrictions on the behavior of the press in general.

Moreover, the more frequently students engage in activities such as posting materials on blogs, the more likely they are to support all manner of free expression across the five separate dimensions studied in FOFA 2006. And finally, with regard to the issue of apathy toward the First Amendment—a measure that registered so low that it startled many educators when they first learned about it in 2004—it appears that the more frequent bloggers tend to develop an attitude that includes more personal thought about First Amendment rights in general. Thus, student bloggers are leading a revolution many of us should be familiar with: it is a revolution that supports free expression rights in general and free press rights in particular.

The Implications of New Media for Democracy

What are the implications of this new media movement on democracy in general and on our rights as Americans in particular? This much is certain: high school students are especially likely to be socialized in ways that promote democracy and celebrate the rights and liberties of all Americans if they engage in an activity that serves as a manifestation of those rights in practice. Student newspapers and other more traditional student media once provided that outlet; unfortunately, they tend to be inherently limited by several factors, including (1) their dependence on advisers and principals to support them with resources, and (2) their dependence on school authorities to help them distribute news to fellow students and the school community as a whole on a regular basis. That dynamic places principals in a position to censor or discourage certain news items, even when they are important and newsworthy. Some principals, caught between a rock and a hard place, may choose to influence (or, in extreme cases, outright censor) the content of student newspapers to avoid the risk of angering parents, superintendents, and others. The adage "better safe than sorry" may be practical, but it does little to promote learning about the value of freedom of expression in the nation's high schools.

In 2006, the more apt adage reads, "If you can't beat 'em, join 'em." High school students have apparently done exactly that, reading and accessing Internet news, then becoming their own editors and publishers through sites such as Myspace.com. School officials have reason to be wary: they cannot condone the dissemination of pornographic materials and other irresponsible activity on the Internet any more than they can condone it in student newspapers or magazines. But the vast majority of what's found on blogs falls within the core protections of the First Amendment, and students who post material online are direct beneficiaries of this robust marketplace of ideas. Those same students who go online and read about news or publish their opinions about it are also among the leading defenders of free expression rights. More effective forms of civic education cannot easily be found.

> "The plaintiffs in the Ithaca High School
> Tattler *censorship case are still working*
> *to preserve future generations' freedom*
> *of speech."*

Former High School Students Are Pursuing a Newspaper Censorship Case in Federal Court

Ithaca Times

The following article from the city newspaper of Ithaca, New York, tells how and why members of the 2005 staff of the high school newspaper Tattler *are still pursuing their lawsuit against the school district that prohibited them from publishing a cartoon satirizing the school's teaching of sex education in health classes. The judge of the federal district court ruled in favor of the school, and although the plaintiffs have now graduated from college, they are appealing to a higher court in order to preserve freedom of the press for future high school students. As of early 2011 this case has not yet been decided. It is considered an important one that may eventually reach the Supreme Court.*

It's been half a decade since eight editors of the Ithaca High School *Tattler* took the city school district to court over claims of censorship and violations of freedom of the press.

But for plaintiffs Andrew Alexander and Rob Ochshorn, the five years have passed very quickly—and, they say, time has not eroded the importance of the issue.

"The meaning of the case has changed very little as the years have gone by," said Ochshorn, who was editor-in-chief of the *Tattler* in 2005, when the lawsuit began. "We believed that free thought and expression were vital to maintain the health of Ithaca High School, especially during a time of unwelcome change, and we haven't wavered in that belief."

A judge ruled in late January [2010] to allow the plaintiffs to go forward in appealing the court's 2009 decision that the *Tattler* paper was a limited public forum and thus is not subject to First Amendment rights. The decision, made in 2nd U.S. Circuit Court of Appeals in New York, seeks to end the current restrictions still in place on the *Tattler*, which are based on the assumption that the paper is not an independent entity and is therefore not subject to full freedom of speech and freedom of press.

So, though they've all graduated from college, five years later and from all corners of the globe—from New York to China—the plaintiffs in the Ithaca High School *Tattler* censorship case are still working to preserve future generations' freedom of speech.

"The plaintiffs are a snapshot in time," said Raymond Schlather, attorney for the case's seven plaintiffs, who has been working on the case pro bono [without charge]. "But the issue still holds, it's still ripe and it will be important to the next generation of editors."

The Finances

But what's also pertinent now is the issue of district spending. The plaintiffs have never been pursuing the case for anything other than principle—they believe in the *Tattler* and what it represents, and they're determined to pass that on, Schlather said.

Though they are not pursuing financial damages, he said, they do seek token damages as required by law.

Adam Goldstein, attorney advocate for the Arlington, Virginia, based Student Press Law Center, which educates high school and college students about their First Amendment rights, said the way he sees things, this case is a massive waste of taxpayer money. "Every day this case goes forward is money wasted," he said. "These are people who have been trusted with public funds; I can't envision why they're still in that position. Nothing you can do with two stick figures [shown in the censored cartoon in various configurations that officials considered obscene] would be worth that kind of money to me as a taxpayer."

How much money? It's unclear, said Schlather. "Let's put it this way," he said. "We're working pro bono on our end, and if you had to add it up the time and put a value on it, it's huge. I've given up keeping track. It's easily well into the six figures."

The suit predates the tenure of Rob Ainslie, ICSD [Ithaca City School District]'s current school board president. Ainslie said that though questions of constitutional law are both interesting and important, the case is not on his list of priorities, as

© Robert Ochshorn.

he and his board deal with an, at minimum, $6 million budget deficit.

"I'm all for free speech, free press," he said. "But on my list of priorities, it's not that not important; it's way back on the back burner."

Ainslie said that in his three years on the board and two as president, the case has never come up as a topic for discussion. He said the district does have insurance that covers a range of legal issues that an organization as large at the ICSD would routinely be exposed to, and it was his impression that they are continuing to fight the legal battle because the insurance carrier wishes to do so.

Is whatever amount of money that has been spent by the district on their end of the suit significant, or is it minute in the face of millions [of dollars]?

"These days, there's no such thing as a minute amount of money," he said. "There's a chance this is going to go above and beyond the allotted attorney retainer. On my dollar, it's not critical and important."

A Broader Look

Goldstein said the broader issue is determining whether the *Tattler* is one of two court-set precedents: a *Tinker* paper, which means that students are afforded First Amendment rights, or *Hazelwood* paper, which means that cocurricular student papers are a limited public forum, where not all First Amendment rights are afforded.

But really, the *Hazelwood* case doesn't hold water, Goldstein said. It was 1988, and things have changed a lot in terms of divorce and teen pregnancy issues. "I don't think that any court today could say with a straight face that 14 year olds don't know

Image on the following pages: The US Supreme Court ruled that Mary Beth Tinker (right) and her brother were allowed to wear black armbands to protest the Vietnam War despite school administrators' objections. Attorney Raymond Schlather argued that the Tattler *case is akin to* Tinker. © Bettmann/Corbis.

about teen pregnancy," he said. He noted that teen pregnancy is a very common topic in today's celebrity news, and the case would likely not have had the same outcome if it were to go before court today.

Tinker holds that public schools are subject to First Amendment laws, and expression is legal so long as it doesn't disrupt the learning environment. Protests in the form of sit-ins and walk-outs are illegal, because they compromise the ability for schools to accomplish their mission of educating students. In this case, no one is accusing that the paper disrupted sex ed classes, Goldstein said.

Schlather said he is working to show that the *Tattler* is a *Tinker* paper; not a *Hazelwood* paper, as the court decided. "*Tinker* says that students don't check their First Amendment rights at the schoolhouse gates," Schlather said. "Editors did not check their First Amendment rights at the Ithaca High School Gates." Schlather said because the *Tattler* is fully extracurricular, 90 percent funded by students through ad sales, and produced on their own cameras and computers and printed offsite, and has a circulation that reaches just as many people outside the school as inside it, it should be recognized as a public forum. . . .

Looking Back

There's nothing like first-hand experience as a learning tool, Ochshorn said. "We all came to an appreciation of First Amendment rights and our role in maintaining [a] representative democracy, as well as the role of newspapers and journalism," he said. "It sounds pretty lofty, but our experience through high school brought it down to . . . terms we could understand."

Alexander, who was news editor and managing editor that year, graduated in May [2009] from the University of Chicago. He's now teaching calculus at a charter school in Arizona. It would be cliche to say [the work done by him and his fellow student journalists] on the paper promoted a sense of leadership, he said. But then, how to describe the monthly workings of the paper's staff? They wrote all 50 to 60 articles, sold all the ads, did all the design work for the 36-or-so-page monthly newspaper. "That ability to run an organization, be in charge of something real, when you're 16, 17, 18 years old, had a profound effect on me and rest of the editors," Alexander said.

Ochshorn said that since high school, he's kept with his interest in journalism. He edited *Kitsch* magazine, a student-run publication in town, and he also worked for the *Cornell Daily Sun* as a student. He said while working within journalism circles through college, the *Tattler* case would often become a topic of conversation. "The lawsuit would come up and we would talk about how the *Tattler* ran," he said.

He said a surprising number of people would say they hadn't bothered working for their high school paper because it was so bad, or they'd say it had been normal for the principal to read through proofs before going to print.

"Anecdotally, there are not many good, in-depth high school papers," he said. "It was a great experience to work for one, and the whole school benefitted from it." Having a strong paper in high school, he said, gave the students a voice to express the discontent they were feeling.

The Specifics

The case has been going on for the better part of five years, Schlather said. The story begins in 2004, he said, when students ran stories that were critical of then-principal Joe Wilson. Things came to a head when Wilson implemented restrictions, which required that all content must be approved by the paper's adviser. Students could file appeals if content was not approved, but the principal and superintendent had final say over what was published.

Later that school year [2004–2005], student editors had planned to run a satirical story on sex ed in health classes, which was to be accompanied by a cartoon which showed a teacher standing in front of a chalkboard depicting nine stick figures in various sexual positions. The cartoon was denied on the grounds that it was obscene.

"Imagine a two-by-three-inch space, and on the board, nine stick figures that look like hieroglyphics," Schlather said.

As a result of the cartoon controversy, the paper's adviser resigned, and the editors were not allowed to publish another issue until a new adviser [was] appointed. But rather than wait, the students decided to publish an underground issue, as had been done in the past in the face of controversy and at points during the Vietnam War. The issue, which looked similar to the *Tattler* but was called *The March Issue*, ran both the cartoon and a story about what had transpired. The students were barred from distributing the paper on school grounds.

By June [2005], the paper had a new adviser, and students asked administration to rescind the guidelines, but they did not. So, Schlather and the plaintiffs filed a suit with the Northern District of New York court in Syracuse, saying that the guidelines imposed by the school were unconstitutional and that the cartoon was not obscene and to not publish it violated the student's first amendment rights.

The court directed both parties to engage in discovery [pretrial disclosure of facts], and they spent much of the next three years taking testimony of everyone involved. The parties submitted their findings to court around the end of 2007, the judge spent 15 months on the decision, and in the spring of 2009, the judge decided the *Tattler* is not an open forum newspaper; rather, that it is a limited public forum. He also decided that the guidelines implemented in 2004 were unconstitutional.

"We got half the loaf," he said. "We were very grateful that the guidelines were decided to be unconstitutional. But if ever there is a high school paper that should enjoy First Amendment rights, to be treated like every other paper, it's the *Tattler*."

When the Wilson-implemented guidelines were ruled unconstitutional by the state court, they were replaced with other, slightly more lenient guidelines. But the current guidelines for the *Tattler* are still tailored to its status as a limited forum, which is what the plaintiffs hope to see changed by the current appeal.

Schlather and his clients then appealed that decision, in hopes that the court will determine the *Tattler* to be an open forum, which is where the case stands today. . . .

The Significance

It's unusual that a case like the *Tattler* lawsuit gets so far, Goldstein said.

"Usually when censorship is this ridiculous, the school pulls it together at some point," he said. "Usually, someone realizes they've made a mistake. It might not be the principal or the superintendent. It could be the school board, or the school attorney who says, 'I can't go in there and defend this with a straight face.' Sooner or later, it should get to someone who says, 'okay, we need to rethink this.'"

But, he said, you need cases like these to remind you of your rights. "There's no impetus to change unless people can see that the way things are working is not good," he said. "You have to show your rights do exist, you have to let people know that things are bad and need to be done differently."

Goldstein said student First Amendment rights violations probably go unpursued most of the time. He said of the 10,000-plus calls he's gotten since starting at the center in 2003 [that] only about three dozen have gone to court. Those are only journalism-related questions, he said, and even then, many people don't know or think to call him.

He said another reason student cases generally don't go very far is that many students don't want to devote all that time to a court case—the plaintiffs in this case are well into college. "They've devoted years of their life to say, 'I have the right to publish this stick-figure cartoon,'" he said. And philosophically, he said, the issue is not new. "There's a line in the Declaration of Independence that says 'men suffer those ills which are sufferable,'" he said.

Students put up with violations of rights all the time, he said. The ones [that] go to court are those insufferable ones—the ones that are either too offensive or too stupid to bear. "This case falls into the latter category," Goldstein said. "It's censorship that is so petty and so meaningless and in some ways it makes it more offensive than an ideological-based censorship."

Ochshorn said the issue is as important as ever. "The First Amendment must be exercised and protected everywhere to allow our democracy to function," Ochshorn said.

Goldstein said the case won't extend student First Amendment rights; it will either [serve] to uphold the rights they have, or it will damage them. "You still have to bring those cases to court," he said. "If rights are so fragile that they can be removed when they are exercised, you need to know that."

| "It is no exaggeration to say that the case
before this Court is the most important
case for the well-being of student
journalism since Hazelwood."

Preventing Students from Publishing Controversial Cartoons Violates Their First Amendment Rights

Joseph P. Esposito et al.

In the following court document, attorneys representing several organizations that favor freedom of the press for high school students argue that a decision of the lower court, which ruled that the Ithaca City School District acted legitimately in censoring a cartoon satirizing Ithaca High School sex education classes, was mistaken and should be reversed by the court of appeals. Protection of constitutional freedoms is vital in public schools, they say, and students have a legal right to express controversial opinions. Moreover, the facts indicate that the reason for the objection to the cartoon was not that it dealt with sex, as was claimed, but that it was critical of the school's teaching methods. Allowing the ruling to stand will mean that student journalists in the future will not be able to publish commentary on significant issues.

This case brings before this Court the important question of whether student journalists have a First Amendment right to critically discuss the teaching methods used in their schools. Curtailment of student journalists' First Amendment right to discuss their schools' curriculum not only hinders the educational purpose of permitting students to act as journalists, [it] also hinders students' education about how and when to question broader issues in society. It also limits the information community members receive about the workings and efficacy of the taxpayer-supported school system they pay for, from some of those in the best position to comment: the student recipients of that education. Accordingly, the Student Press Law Center ("SPLC"), the Journalism Education Association ("JEA"), and the National Scholastic Press Association ("NSPA"), respectfully submit this *amici curiae* [friends of the court] brief in support of Plaintiff-Appellant R.O., a minor, who brings this case through his parent and guardian, Jonathan Ochshorn.

The decision of the court below raises two key issues. First, does a school violate student journalists' First Amendment rights when it prevents a student-run newspaper from publishing an otherwise lawful political cartoon critical of the school's sex education program? Second, can a school prevent dissemination of the cartoon by an independent student publication funded privately and created off-campus? The SPLC, JEA, and NSPA urge reversal of the lower court's decision, which upheld the school's censorship of the cartoon at issue in both the school newspaper and the independent publication. . . .

The speech at issue here is a cartoon parodying a Health 101 class, a mandatory class in which sex education was taught. The cartoon shows a teacher standing at the front of the classroom near a blackboard. The blackboard shows barely discernible stick figures in various sexual positions, and [it] states, "Test on Monday." The cartoon was clearly satirical commentary about the school's sex education curriculum. But for the school's censorship of the cartoon, the cartoon would have accompanied an article that was published which examined the school's sex education teaching methods, including the use of comical skits that promoted abstinence.

The school administration censored the cartoon in two publications. The school first censored the cartoon in the school newspaper, *The Tattler*. *The Tattler* is a publication created and distributed within the school, but it is not part of the school's curriculum, and it has very limited oversight by school officials. All content decisions have traditionally been made by the student editorial staff. The school subsequently censored the cartoon by prohibiting distribution within the school of an independent student newspaper published off-campus, *The March Issue*, which contained the cartoon.

Censoring Criticism of Teaching Methods

As this Court has previously noted [in] *Eisner v. Stamford Bd. of Educ.*, "[a] public school is undoubtedly a 'marketplace of ideas.'" Schools should foster critical thinking skills and challenge students to think "outside the box." In light of the importance that sex education can have on students' lives, the effectiveness of the school's teaching methods is an appropriate topic for a student newspaper. However, if a school censors criticism of its methods and courses, it not only abridges the First Amendment rights of its student journalists, it undermines the educational purpose of operating a student-run newspaper. By permitting the school to censor this material, the District Court's decision threatens to significantly curtail the ability of student journalists to analyze significant issues relating to their education and school administration.

Affirming the District Court's ruling would grant school administrators the authority to unduly restrict student speech analyzing and criticizing key issues affecting the school.

It has long been acknowledged that "'vigilant protection of constitutional freedoms is nowhere more vital than in the community of [our] schools,'" *Guiles v. Marineau*. The education of America's youngest citizens must include teaching the ability to analyze and challenge the world around them. Schools, therefore, "may not be enclaves of totalitarianism," *Tinker v. Des Moines*. The Supreme Court has made clear that students are citizens protected by the Constitution, and that they do not lose those protections simply because they are in school. Absent "a specific showing of constitutionally valid reasons to regulate their speech," students' First Amendment speech should not be "confined to the expression of those sentiments that are officially approved." . . .

Regulations of Student Journalism

The Supreme Court has plainly stated that neither "students [nor] teachers shed their constitutional rights to freedom of speech or expression at the schoolhouse gate," *Tinker*. The state, in the person of school officials, may not prohibit speech based on an "undifferentiated fear or apprehension of disturbance." On the contrary, "[a]ny word spoken in class, in the lunchroom, or on the campus, that deviates from the views of another person may start an argument or cause a disturbance. But our Constitution says we must take this risk . . . and our history says that it is this sort of hazardous freedom—this kind of openness—that is the basis of our national strength. . . ."

The Tattler cartoon is precisely the type of speech that the *Tinker* Court meant to protect, because it encourages public discourse and fosters a marketplace of ideas. The cartoon was a satirical commentary meant to accompany an article discussing pro-abstinence skits in Health class that used "exaggerat[ed]" and "comical" analogies to persuade students to abstain from sex. The school claimed that the cartoon would be "inconsistent with the educational mission and pedagogical concerns of the District"; the lower court concluded that such concerns justified the censorship. In fact, neither the school nor the court below had any basis for determining that the cartoon would be disruptive

The Ithaca City School District's Argument for Censorship

The Defendants' decision . . . to deny publication of the sexual stick figures drawing was reasonably related to a legitimate pedagogical concern. . . . Mr. [Joe] Wilson [the principal] upheld the Faculty Adviser's decision, finding the drawing obscene and not suitable for immature audiences, and consequently inconsistent with the educational mission and concerns of the District. This concern was exacerbated by the fact that the drawing was intended to accompany an article about the ICSD's health education programs, focusing on how sex is being taught in Ithaca schools, which Mr. Wilson felt would give impressionable students, parents and the community the impression that sex was not a serious subject in ICSD [Ithaca City School District] schools and that the District was promoting recreational or irresponsible sex among school-aged children.

Superintendent [Judith] Pastel, who upheld both decisions, testified that she considered the drawing obscene, and that its distribution would be offensive to many students and confusing to others, particularly those immature students whose understanding of and views about sexual relations are not yet fully formed. In the context of the dangerous sexual behavior young ICSD students were engaged in at this time, it was incumbent upon Superintendent Pastel and the District to put forth a consistent message about sex. . . . Understanding that *The Tattler* would be read by students as young as twelve or thirteen years old, as well as many parents and members of the Ithaca community, the ICSD decided that such a lewd depiction of sexual relations in a District newspaper could not be allowed.

Memorandum of Law in Support of Defendants'
Motion for Summary Judgment, R.O. v. Ithaca
City School District, *US District Court,*
Northern District of New York,
April 13, 2007.

because of its sexual content. On the contrary, *The Tattler* regularly published articles containing sexual innuendo or references to sex. But because the cartoon satirized the school's sex education curriculum, it was censored. The lower court's decision should be overturned because it wrongly concludes that schools may censor students' legitimate political commentary based on unsubstantiated fear.

The Cartoon Is Protected Speech

As this Court has stated [in *Guiles*], a student may freely express his opinion, "even on controversial subjects . . . if he does so without materially and substantially interfer[ing] with the requirements of appropriate discipline in the operation of the school and without colliding with the rights of others." The cartoon at issue here is protected speech that does not fall within the narrow exceptions established by the Supreme Court and this Circuit. . . .

A sex education class in session. The US Supreme Court has found that a school is "a marketplace of ideas" and therefore a school's sex education program is an appropriate topic for a school newspaper. © AP Images/Kevin P. Casey.

It is plain from the record that the school's concern that *The Tattler* cartoon was obscene or would lead to risky sexual behavior was exaggerated or pretextual. *The Tattler* regularly published articles and opinion pieces containing sexual speech. For example, the February 2005 issue of *The Tattler* included a point/counterpoint about the virtues of monogamy, and very graphic reviews of a sexually explicit movie. The cartoon at issue here—which was censored from the very same February 2005 edition of *The Tattler*—was not prurient, but—as journalists in America have done since our country's founding—used criticism and satire to make a point. Unlike the other *Tattler* articles that more casually referred to sex, however, the cartoon was satire accompanying a substantive article about Ithaca High School's sex education curriculum. . . .

The *Tattler* Cartoon Is Not Subject to *Hazelwood* Scrutiny

In view of the facts in the record, *The Tattler* constituted a designated public forum. At a minimum, the record evidence should have precluded the lower court from ruling on summary judgment that the newspaper was something other than a designated public forum. Regardless, having ruled that the newspaper was a limited public forum, the court below then compounded its error by proceeding to engage in a *Hazelwood* analysis, which applies only when a forum has not been established.

It is plain error to apply *Hazelwood*'s reduced level of First Amendment protection (the "legitimate pedagogical concern" standard rather than the *Tinker* "material and substantial disruption" standard) to a public forum newspaper. . . . But even under *Hazelwood*—which is not applicable here—censorship of the cartoon was unconstitutional. In *Hazelwood*, the Supreme Court permitted schools to censor school-sponsored speech in non-public forums where the censorship is "reasonably related to legitimate pedagogical concerns," including speech that "might reasonably be perceived to advocate drug or alcohol use, irresponsible sex, or conduct otherwise inconsistent with 'the shared values of a civilized society,'" *Hazelwood*. However, the Court in *Hazelwood* made clear that "when the decision to censor a school-sponsored publication, theatrical production, or other vehicle of student expression has no valid education purpose," the First Amendment is implicated and judicial intervention is required to protect students' constitutional rights.

The school's claim that it had a valid educational purpose for censoring *The Tattler* cartoon finds no support in the facts. The school maintains that the cartoon advocates irresponsible sex by minors. The opposite is true. . . .

The District Court's *Tinker* analysis was fatally flawed because the court required absolutely no causal link between the censorship and the problem sought to be addressed. The court simply went through a litany of the school's concerns about student sexual behavior and then concluded summarily, "Defendants reasonably concluded that the cartoon would have a harmful effect on the students and disrupt school activities." This is far from the tight cause/effect analysis that *Tinker* demands. If not reversed, the District Court's overly deferential analysis will send the message that, when a school has a concern about any social problem (pregnancy, drug use, violence), it may censor at will any mention of that topic simply by asserting that the speech is counterproductive to solving the problem.

First Amendment Violation

Like the simple cloth armband Mary Beth Tinker made at home and wore to Harding Middle School in Des Moines, Iowa, 45 years ago, *The March Issue* was an independently produced means of communication neither funded by nor attributable to Ithaca High School. The speech it contained was entirely the work of the student publishers.

Leaving aside whether censorship of the school-funded *Tattler* was permissible, the school violated well-established law and the students' basic constitutional rights as citizens to speak independently and report the news by preventing distribution of the privately produced and funded *The March Issue*.

First, the District Court erred by deciding that the school could exclude *The March Issue* under [*Bethel School District v.*] *Fraser* because it was obscene ("no reasonable fact finder could conclude that the images were anything but obscene"). In fact, the exact opposite is true. As discussed above, the cartoon was offered in the best journalistic tradition of criticism and satire, and was not offered for prurient reasons. The school's problem is not with the use of stick figures to illustrate sex—it is with the use of stick figures to illustrate a viewpoint with which it disagrees. . . .

The Most Important Free Press Case Since *Hazelwood*

It is no exaggeration to say that the case before this Court is the most important case for the well-being of student journalism since *Hazelwood*. When *Hazelwood* was decided, critics feared—presciently, as it turned out—that school administrators would abuse the latitude afforded by that ruling to censor material simply because it displeased them.

Fortunately, there are fail-safes to spare student journalists from the "censorship tsunami" that is *Hazelwood*. One is to obtain public forum designation for the publication, so that it no longer may be censored on the basis of a thinly documented "pedagogical concern." The other is to publish an independently funded newspaper unaffiliated with the school. The students at Ithaca High School attempted to take advantage of both of these fail-safes to publish substantive material advancing the dialogue on matters of public concern—the highest and best calling of journalism. In attempting to communicate most effectively with their audience, they made the editorial judgment to include an element of satire to dramatize their point, just as professional journalists have done to great effect for centuries. . . .

If the Court tells the students of Ithaca High School that they had no legally protected right to satirize the ineffectiveness of a school policy—the effectiveness of which the school itself is telling this Court is *a matter of life and death*—then the "chill" of intimidation that student journalists already feel when they bravely take up a critical pen against their elders will turn into a deep freeze. Important stories about the inner workings of schools—stories which student journalists, in this era of eroding professional news organizations, are alone positioned to document and share—will never see the light of day. Vulnerable students will be exposed to life-altering disciplinary sanctions for "crimes" no greater than truthfully blowing the whistle on the shortcomings of their schools. We need not speculate that this will occur, because 22 years of experience with *Hazelwood* demonstrates that it assuredly will.

The SPLC, JEA, and NSPA respectfully urge the Court to reverse the District Court's ruling that the First Amendment did not protect *The Tattler* cartoon or *The March Issue* from censorship.

Organizations to Contact

The editors have compiled the following list of organizations concerned with the issues debated in this book. The descriptions are derived from materials provided by the organizations.

Center for Scholastic Journalism

School of Journalism and Mass Communication, Kent State University, Kent, OH 44242
website: http://jmc.kent.edu/csj

The Center for Scholastic Journalism at Kent State University offers support for high school and middle school journalism advisers and their students. Its website includes information about legal and ethical issues, curricular help, and lesson plans, plus a blog.

Columbia Scholastic Press Association (CSPA)

Columbia University, Mail Code 5711, New York, NY 10027-6902
(212) 854-9400 • Fax: (212) 854-9401
e-mail: cspa@columbia.edu
website: www.columbia.edu/cu/cspa

The Columbia Scholastic Press Association is a program of the Columbia University School of Journalism. It works with high school and college student editors and faculty advisers to produce student newspapers, magazines, yearbooks and online media. Its website contain news and contest information, plus information about books on journalism that it publishes.

Dow Jones News Fund (DJNF)

PO Box 300, Princeton, NJ 08543-0300
Phone: (609) 452-2820 • Fax: (609) 520-5804

e-mail: djnf@dowjones.com
website: www.newsfund.org

The Dow Jones News Fund is a national foundation supported by Dow Jones and others within the news industry. It emphasizes education for students and educators as part of its mission to promote careers in journalism. It operates several high school-level and college-level grant programs. Its website features information about its publications and projects, including high school workshops.

First Amendment Center

Vanderbilt University, 1207 18th Avenue S, Nashville, TN 37212
(615) 727-1600 • Fax: (615) 727-1319
e-mail: info@fac.org
website: www.firstamendmentcenter.org

The First Amendment Center is a nonpartisan program of the Freedom Forum that provides education to the public and groups including First Amendment scholars and experts, educators, government policy makers, legal experts and students. Its website includes news, information, and commentary on First Amendment issues as well as detailed reports about US Supreme Court cases involving the First Amendment.

J-Ideas

Department of Journalism, Ball State University, Muncie, IN 47306
(765) 285-8923
website: http://jideas.org

J-Ideas was developed at Ball State University to develop and encourage excellence in high school journalism through on-site activities, tailored programs, distance learning, and digital activities and scholarship. Its goal is to foster First Amendment and civic awareness. Its website includes teaching tools, news, interviews, and information about the DVDs it produces.

High School Journalism Initiative
11690B Sunrise Valley Drive, Reston VA 20191-1409
Fax: 703-453-1139
website: www.hsj.org

The High School Journalism Initiative is a program of the American Society of News Editors (ASNE). Its website features extensive information and resources for high school journalists, including advice about online publication and lesson plans for journalism teachers.

My High School Journalism
website: http://my.hsj.org

My High School Journalism is a free Web hosting service for youth news sites, presently connected to more than 3,500 of them. It is a program of the High School Journalism Initiative (see above). It allows students to publish stories, photos, podcasts, video, and other multimedia journalism online, and its site features *The National Edition,* carrying the best in teen journalism.

National Scholastic Press Association (NSPA)
2221 University Avenue SE, Suite 121, Minneapolis, MN 55414
Phone: 612-625-8335 • Fax: 612-626-0720
website: www.studentpress.org/nspa

The NSPA is a nonprofit educational association that provides journalism education services to students, teachers, media advisers, and others throughout the United States and in other countries. Its website includes long articles on topics that help student media organizations function, plus an online collection showcasing some of the best work in student media by its members.

National Youth Rights Association (NYRA)

1101 15th Street NW, Suite 200, Washington, DC, 20005
(202) 835-1739
website: www.youthrights.org

NYRA is a youth-led national nonprofit organization dedicated to fighting for the civil rights and liberties of young people. NYRA has more than 7,000 members representing all 50 states. It seeks to lower the voting age, lower the drinking age, repeal curfew laws, and protect student rights.

Poynter Institute

801 Third Street S, St. Petersburg, FL 33701
(727) 821-9494
website: www.poynterextra.org/centerpiece/highschool

The Poynter Institute is a school dedicated to teaching and inspiring journalists and media leaders. It teaches those who manage, edit, produce, program, report, write, blog, photograph, and design, whether they belong to news organizations or work as independent entrepreneurs, as well as students in middle school, high school, and college. Its website offers articles and links for high school journalists.

Quill and Scroll

School of Journalism and Mass Communication, University of Iowa
100 Adler Journalism Building, Iowa City, IA 52242
(319) 335-3457 • Fax: (319) 335-3989
e-mail: quill-scroll@uiowa.edu
website: www.uiowa.edu/~quill-sc

Quill and Scroll International Honorary Society for High School Journalists was organized in 1926 at the University of Iowa for the purpose of encouraging and recognizing individual student achievement in journalism and scholastic publication. It has granted school charters to more than 14,267 high schools.

Its website includes information about awards, contests, and scholarships, as well as a few articles from its magazine *Quill and Scroll.*

Reporters Committee for Freedom of the Press

1101 Wilson Blvd., Suite 1100, Arlington, VA 22209
(800) 336-4243
website: www.rcfp.org

The Reporters Committee for Freedom of the Press is a non-profit organization dedicated to providing free legal assistance to journalists. It is a major national and international resource on free speech issues, and it disseminates information in a variety of forms, including a quarterly legal review, a weekly newsletter, a twenty-four-hour hotline, and various handbooks on media law issues. Many of its publications are online at its website.

Student Press Law Center (SPLC)

1101 Wilson Blvd., Suite 1100, Arlington, VA 22209-2275
(703) 807-1904
website: www.splc.org

The SPLC is the nation's only legal assistance agency devoted exclusively to educating high school and college journalists about the rights and responsibilities embodied in the First Amendment, and to support the student news media in their struggle to cover important issues free from censorship. The Center provides free legal advice and information as well as low-cost educational materials for student journalists on a wide variety of legal topics.

For Further Reading

Books

Kenneth Dautrich, David A. Yalof, and Mark Jose López, *The Future of the First Amendment: The Digital Media, Civic Education, and Free Expression Rights in America's High Schools.* Lanham, MD: Rowman & Littlefield, 2008.

Joan DelFattore, *Knowledge in the Making: Academic Freedom and Free Speech in America's Schools and Universities.* New Haven, CT: Yale University Press, 2010.

Anne Profitt Depre, *Speaking Up: The Unintended Costs of Free Speech in Public Schools.* Cambridge, MA: Harvard University Press, 2009.

Garrett Epps, *Freedom of the Press: The First Amendment: Its Constitutional History and the Contemporary Debate.* Amherst, NY: Prometheus Books, 2008.

Freedom Forum, *Death by Cheeseburger: High School Journalism in the 1990s and Beyond.* Arlington, VA: Freedom Forum, 1994.

Scott E. Gant, *We're All Journalists Now: The Transformation of the Press and Reshaping of the Law in the Internet Age.* New York: Free Press, 2007.

Jesulon S.R. Gibbs, *Student Speech on the Internet: The Role of First Amendment Protections.* El Paso, TX: LFB Scholarly Publishing, 2010.

Louis E. Inglehart, *Press Law and Press Freedom for High School Publications: Court Cases and Related Decisions.* Santa Barbara, CA: Praeger, 1986.

Nicholas D. Kristof, *Freedom of the High School Press.* Lanham, MD: University of America, 1984.

Jamin B. Raskin, *We the Students: Supreme Court Cases for and About Students.* Washington, DC: CQ Press, 2008.

Jim Streisel, *High School Journalism: A Practical Guide.* Jefferson, NC: McFarland, 2007.

Student Press Law Center, *Law of the Student Press.* Washington, DC: Student Press Law Center, 2008.

Periodicals and Internet Sources

Teresa J. Boggs, "The First Amendment Rights of High School Students and Their Student Newspapers," Thesis, West Virginia University, 2005.

Tyler Buller, "Stirring the Pot," *American School Board Journal,* June 2010.

"High School Journalism Matters," Newspaper Association of America, 2008. www.naafoundation.org/upload/foundation _pdf/journalism-matters-exec-summary.pdf.

Amelia Jimenez, "High School Censorship: Striking a Balance," *Pennsylvania Patriot-News*, April 19, 2009. www.pennlive .com/editorials/index.ssf/2009/04/high_school_censorship _strikin.html.

Richard Just, "Unmuzzling High School Journalists," *Washington Post*, January 12, 2008. www.washingtonpost .com/wp-dyn/content/article/2008/01/11/ AR2008011102775.html.

Kathleen Klink, "Freeing the Student Press for Their Good and Ours," *School Administrator*, April 2002.

Jamie Loo, "Stevenson Student Journalists Defend Newspaper," *Post-Exchange,* December 18, 2009. www.mccormick foundation.org/civics/programs/post-exchange/Article -Stevenson_statesman_schoolboard.aspx.

McCormick Foundation, "Freedom of Speech and the Press in the Information Age," 2008. www.jamesmadison.com /lessons/freedom_of_speech_and_the_press.pdf.

Michael Moore, "Join My High School Newspaper," *Daily Kos*, February 18, 2011. www.dailykos.com/story/2011/02/18 /946802/-Join-My-High-School-Newspaper.

Gene Policinski, "We're Strangling High School Free Speech, Press," American Press Institute, August 9, 2007. www .americanpressinstitute.org/pages/resources/2007/08/ were_strangling_high_school_fr.

Greg Toppo, "Students Say Press Freedoms Go Too Far," *USA Today*, January 30, 2005.

Jodi Wilgoren, "Lessons High School Students Learn About Freedom of the Press," *New York Times*, November 17, 1999.

Index